FROM
ROSES
TO
TERROR

A Journal of Being **Hunted by a Stalker**

Di McDonald

Forward by James R. Fitzgerald, former FBI agent

GRAMMAR
FACTORY
— EST? 2013 —

Published by Grammar Factory Publishing,
an imprint of MacMillan Company Limited.

Grammar Factory Publishing
MacMillan Company Limited
25 Telegram Mews, 39th Floor, Suite 3906
Toronto, Ontario, Canada
M5V 3Z1

www.grammarfactory.com

McDonald, Di.
From Roses to Terror: A Journal of Being Hunted by a Stalker / Di McDonald.

Paperback ISBN 978-1-998528-15-8
eBook ISBN 978-1-998528-16-5
Audiobook ISBN 978-1-998528-38-7

1. TRU000000 TRUE CRIME / General.
2. SEL049000 SELF-HELP / Safety & Security / General.
3. SOC063000 SOCIAL SCIENCE / Privacy & Surveillance.

Production Credits
Cover design by Designerbility
Book production and editorial services
by Grammar Factory Publishing
Author photo on back cover by Simon Winter, ABC

Grammar Factory's Carbon Neutral Publishing Commitment
Grammar Factory Publishing is proud to be neutralizing the carbon
footprint of all printed copies of its authors' books printed by or ordered
directly through Grammar Factory or its affiliated companies through
the purchase of Gold Standard-Certified International Offsets.

Disclaimer
This book is based on true events. However, in order to protect the
privacy of individuals involved, some names, locations and identifying
details have been changed or omitted. Any resemblance to persons
living or deceased, outside of the intended depictions, is purely coincidental.
The content of this book is presented with the utmost respect for all those
affected by the events described. While every effort has been made to
ensure accuracy, certain aspects of the narrative may reflect the author's
interpretation or be reconstructed from publicly available records,
personal interviews and other sources. Readers are advised that the book
contains content that may be distressing. Discretion is strongly advised.

WHAT IF SOMEONE
WANTS YOU DEAD...

BUT YOU LIVE TO TELL...

Here is my story...

*To all victims of stalking, domestic
violence or any sort of violence.*

*Trust your gut instincts;
they will never fail you.*

CONTENTS

FOREWORD

I'VE SPENT OVER thirty-one years in US law enforcement. That includes twenty years in the Federal Bureau of Investigation, with the last twelve years therein as a supervisory special agent, criminal profiler, and forensic linguist. I retired from the Bureau in 2007, but remain very active in various ongoing professional endeavors, while occasionally working on criminal cases with police departments and other investigative agencies. Over the last nearly two decades, most of these cases involved crime-oriented language analysis, or Forensic Linguistics. In 2019 a criminal investigative matter in, of all places, Australia, came my way. Little did I know then, it may just hold the distinction of being the last criminal case I ever officially worked.

The first case of my FBI profiling career was the UNABOM investigation. In 1996 it took me (literally) to a small cabin in the mountains of the US state of Montana in which my analysis of a lengthy Manifesto, and other documents, led to the eventual arrest of a notorious serial bomber. The last criminal case of my linguistics career—to date, anyway—took me (virtually) to the

Australian state of Victoria. And once again, my language evidence analysis led to another arrest, this time of a notorious serial stalker. These two cases, separated by twenty-three years and half a planet, differ in many ways. Nonetheless, they represent noteworthy book-ends to my forensic linguistic crime-solving career. And, I should add, I am equally proud of both.

Di McDonald is the reason, even if indirectly, I became involved in the Victoria stalking matter. She was the victim—no, make that *survivor*—of several years of being actively harassed, threatened, and psychologically traumatized by an anonymous individual. Of course, Di didn't choose this role—being stalked by an unknown serial predator—but unfortunately, through no fault of her own, she found herself living through this all-too-personal crime drama. Among other issues, the case involved a series of anonymous writings, some threatening, some obscene—all covered with the linguistic fingerprints of the stalker, if only someone trained in language analysis could identify them.

Di enlisted Victoria Police, and thanks to a newly assigned detective senior constable who just happened to have seen *Manhunt: Unabomber*, a true-crime television series about my work on that case (in which my character, coincidently, was portrayed by an Australian actor), my help was requested, and I was brought on board. Through my language analysis, in which I was able to link the anonymous writings to the perpetrator—and thanks to the dogged determination and dedication of the detective senior constable and her team—the case was soon resolved, for good.

In *From Roses to Terror*, Di McDonald describes many fascinating aspects of her life, centering on the unusual, if not unlikely, legalistic collaboration that led to the

FBI's UNABOM profiler/forensic linguist—that's me—helping to put yet another bad guy in prison; this time, an Australian prison.

However, *From Roses to Terror* is not about me. It's not about the detective. It's not even about the stalker. It's about the author, Di McDonald, and in her own voice. It's about the heavy cross she was forced to carry, mostly on her own, for long segments of her unforeseen years-long journey into the crime victimization abyss.

During those several years in which Di was intermittently mentally violated by her unknown stalker, she clearly suffered personally, professionally, financially, and emotionally. She became desperate on occasion, even with the ongoing support of her family and friends. At times, it seemed almost impossible for her to continue. Her harasser would not leave her alone. He was persistent, and he was cruel. Even when Di's very good friend suddenly died, the stalker anonymously, but publicly, blamed Di for the death. Many of us would have folded, capitulated, and/or surrendered.

However, Di was persistent too, and she maintained her belief in herself and in the cause of bringing her stalker to justice. In *From Roses to Terror*, Di shares with the reader her travails into the valleys of deep and utter frustration. But you'll also read how she climbed back out of these valleys, slowly at first, but ultimately successfully.

From Roses to Terror is as real as it gets. I know true crime, and this is as true as it gets, from multiple important perspectives. These include descriptions of the crimes themselves; Di's emotional roller coaster ride along the way after each new stalking incident; and the seemingly endless investigative process, with the police having to tell her, over and over again, 'Well, we don't have quite enough evidence for an arrest yet.' But Di's patience, fortitude, and ultimately her strong sense of self eventually paid off. That prior victim then morphed into present survivor mode.

Di McDonald walked the walk and now she talks the talk. From a victim's pain and anguish to a survivor's eventual healing, if not prospering. But Di doesn't stop there. Since her stalker was finally brough to justice, she has become very active in various government, social, and political causes in Australia to prevent other women, or for that matter anyone, from suffering, as she did, at the hands of a stalker and/or a domestic abuser. She's working hard to improve policy and laws in Australia. She will succeed too. I'm sure of it.

From Roses to Terror is an important book. Academics, law enforcement professionals, government officials, and the mental health community should read it and become familiar with the pathology of a stalker, as well as the impacts on victims, families, and friends. The general public will also benefit and learn from this book, and not only about stalking and how to survive it, but also about courage, resilience, and fighting for justice, even when the case feels hopeless.

When interviewing Di on my *Cold Red* podcast and listening to her tell her story to our audience (some of the facts which I already knew, but others of which I did not), I found myself uttering a simple term as we were about to sign off. I didn't think of it in advance. It wasn't preplanned. It wasn't in my notes. It materialized spontaneously, yet seriously.

That term was 'Di McDonald-Strong'. I meant it to apply to a person or a group with a certain fearlessness, purposefulness, and determination to meet clear objectives in their lives, despite certain hardships, no matter how seemingly difficult. Yes, I borrowed the term from other uses of '-Strong' to refer to people and places that have suffered through very difficult violent events but managed to survive—and thrive—in the long run. That's what I saw, and heard, and came to know and respect about this person. She is Di McDonald-Strong and personally demonstrates all the positivity the word 'strong' connotes.

The strength of Di McDonald is replete throughout *From Roses to Terror*. I'm honored to now be a part of her book, but more importantly, to now be a part of her life, even if half a world apart. Upon reading Di's words, you'll too learn of her strength, and I have no doubt you will become stronger for it. And you do *not* have to be a criminal profiler or forensic linguist to realize the true impact of her story.

JAMES R. FITZGERALD,
Supervisory Special Agent, FBI (Ret.)
Criminal Profiler, Forensic Linguist
Author, Academic, Media Consultant, Podcaster

PROLOGUE

ON SUNDAY 14 June, 2015, I swallowed every pill I could find in my house. I was on Endep for fibromyalgia and there are fifty little yellow tablets in a packet—I took them all. I had changed to another medication for my fibromyalgia, so I took all those pills as well. It wasn't easy; I kept wanting to vomit. But I persevered. I got all the pills down and kept them down. What kept me going was thinking about the nightmare I had brought into my life and the lives of my family and friends—a nightmare that was getting worse. I had tried again and again to stop it, but nothing had worked. I was the ultimate target of the nightmare; I thought that if I was gone, the nightmare would be gone. The people I loved would have peace, they would be safe, and all the yelling and screaming would stop. After I was gone, I thought my family and friends would be grateful that the turmoil had stopped. I didn't leave a note, I didn't explain why I was doing it. I thought everyone would know and be happy.

So I lay down to rest, praying I wouldn't see the morning.

But I did...

PART 1

THE STALKER, THE DETECTIVE AND THE FBI AGENT

FIRST DATES
AND RED FLAGS

THE NIGHTMARE BEGAN on an ordinary day in October 2014.

I'd been through some major life changes in the previous few years. In 2011 I was living in Mooroopna in regional Victoria when my marriage broke down. My daughters, Amity and Rhiannon, came to live with me but I was saddened that my son, Sam, chose to live with his father. At the same time, my parents were not getting any younger and their health was failing. After one too many mad dashes down the highway to Melbourne to help them out with one thing or another, I decided I had to move back there. Sitting in my childhood home in Blackburn South one Sunday afternoon, I went through the real estate section in the newspaper. Mum and Dad didn't realise what I was doing; I was looking for somewhere I could afford to live without taking out too big a mortgage or, at the very least, paying too much rent! Three suburbs stood out: Craigieburn, Epping and Lalor.

At the time I was working at a Big W department store in Shepparton. When I got back home and went into work the next day, there was a poster up on the notice-board announcing that a new store would be opening in Craigieburn. How amazing that I had already identified Craigieburn as a potential new home for me! I thought it was a sign, so I applied for a transfer. I also learnt that my first boss at Big W, whom I loved working for, had applied for a transfer to the new store. Perfect, I thought, this was meant to be. Life would be more settled now.

With the transfer approved, I started looking for a house in Craigieburn. I searched for months and months, and meanwhile I had to drive up and down the high-way between Mooroopna and Craigieburn every day as I helped to set up the new store. It was a long day, start-ing at 4.30 am and not finishing until I got home at 7:30 pm. Then, one Saturday, after inspecting yet another unsuitable property, the agent gave me the address of a house that might be coming on the market soon. I drove past and loved the quaint little cottage. After a meeting at the house with the agent, he called me the following Tuesday to say the house was on the market. I put in an offer straight away, and it was accepted. Settlement was completed in December 2013 and we all began to move in. Amity put herself into further study, and I enrolled Rhiannon in the local secondary school. It was hard mov-ing away from my Sam, but we made it work. And there would be no more long days and long drives!

I'D STARTED DATING after my divorce, and sometimes had men ask me out while I was at work. One day in October 2014 I helped out a guy called Marty. He was so grateful for the help I'd given him that he came back with a rose and a handwritten note for me. I'd had a hard day and appreciated the sentiment, but told him he didn't need to do that; I was just doing my job as the front-end

When I first met Marty, he presented
me with this 'Greek Angel'

supervisor. My work colleagues had a field day handing around the note and put the rose in water for me so I could put it on my desk.

The attention didn't stop there. Marty kept coming into the store to say hi. He asked me out for coffee, and I kept saying no, but my work colleagues said, 'Go, what's the harm?' So I took the tentative step of having a coffee with Marty at a place in Craigieburn Central, the shopping centre where my Big W store was located. Then I discovered that one of my work friends knew him, and said he was a good guy who would spoil me rotten. So, on her advice, I accepted a dinner invitation. After all, as my colleague said, if it didn't work out I could just move on, right?

Over dinner, I discovered that Marty had a son and daughter who were both in their thirties, as well as a twelve-year-old daughter. He also said he was retired and lived alone. I was a bit shocked to discover he was sixty-two—twelve years older than me—but I pushed aside my apprehension and went on a few more dinners with Marty, whom I found to be quite charming. He was kind, thoughtful and respectful—unlike other men I'd known—and was always well presented. He dressed impeccably and never had a hair out of place. We began to see each other regularly.

It was late October before I took Marty over to meet my best friend, Cathie Maney. I had met Cathie when she started dating my friend Frank Howson, who wrote the musical *Dream Lover*, but it was Cathie and I who ended up being inseparable. We became great friends after I moved back to Melbourne, and we were always out together seeing bands or meeting up for a drink at her local, the Winelarder. Cathie came on road trips with me and other friends to see our favourite musicians play. There was never a dull moment with Cathie. We were always in fits of laughter and creating chaos. Life was good, and I loved being back in Melbourne.

When I told Cathie about Marty, she was worried that he wouldn't like her; she thought he might think she was a bit crazy—I mean, she was an artist and a bit boisterous and even eccentric at times. After I introduced them, Marty sent me a lovely text message about Cath, and I sent her a screen shot of it. It said *'Sweetheart, pass my thanks and appreciation on to Cathie for taking such a beautiful, loving photo of us ... I think the picture says it all xox.'.* I told her, *'Marty likes you,'* and her response was, *'That's good, as if he wants you, he unfortunately gets me lol.'* Everything seemed to be going smoothly.

Happy times with Cathie at the Winelarder

Even though Marty and I were spending more and more time together, Cathie and I still hung out quite a bit and even went on a road trip to Traralgon with a couple of other girlfriends to see one of our favourite performers, Daryl Braithwaite. When I went back to work after our weekend away, I discovered Marty had left me flowers and a note that said they were for *'just being me'*. It seemed I was never far from his thoughts.

The following week we all went out to see my friend Jimmy perform with his band Wired. It was Cathie, me, Marty and his friend Ted. Marty loved the band so much that we went to see them again a couple of weeks later. In November we went to the Winelarder again to see friends perform. I picked up the tambourine and Cathie and I provided some backing vocals. We also went to see Kate Ceberano, whose bass player was a friend of mine, performing in Craigieburn. On Melbourne Cup Day,

Marty, Cathie and I went to the Elwood Food & Wine Bar for lunch. We had a lovely day, all dressed up with our hats on. Life was good, but not without its sad moments.

My father had died in July of that year. He collapsed in the shower one day and was taken to hospital, where we nearly lost him. He eventually went home, but never fully recovered. After a few months he was admitted to hospital again, where he spent the last five weeks of his life.

My beloved pooch, Gypsy, had also become sick earlier in 2014. She had been my world since 2004. She came everywhere with me, and adored the car, hanging her head out or just looking out the window. Sometimes she even wore sunglasses. The day after our lovely Melbourne Cup lunch she finally passed away. Even though she had been sick for months, losing her still hurt. Agreeing to have her put down was the hardest decision I had ever had to make; it broke my heart. The vet gave me a beautiful chocolate mink blanket to wrap Gypsy in so I could take her home afterwards in privacy and comfort. At home, Gypsy and I spent ages cuddling on the couch. Marty came over and dug a beautiful grave for Gypsy. He even said a few lovely words about her. Marty was becoming part of my inner circle and even cared about silly sentimental things like having a little 'funeral' for my dog. It seemed like I had found a good man.

Or was Marty too good to be true?

In November my friend Robyn was coming to Melbourne to see her youngest son. She was keen to meet Marty, as I'd only gone out with one man since 2012 and she wanted to see what was so special about this one. Marty invited Robyn over to his place for dinner, and Rhiannon was coming as well. Robyn had to travel all the way from Albury in New South Wales, which is a long drive, and unfortunately she was extremely late. Marty

TOP Gypsy with her shades on, catching the breeze

BOTTOM Gypsy's grave, dug by Marty

was cooking us all steaks on the barbecue and became increasingly frustrated as the hour got later and later and we were still waiting for Robyn. When she finally showed up, Marty put on his happy face and kept playing 'Songbird' by Fleetwood Mac over and over again. He said it was his song for me, but Robyn found it a bit strange.

After we all ate the delicious meal Marty had cooked for us, Rhiannon said she had arranged to meet up with her friends. She asked me to drive her, but Robyn offered to take her and then she would continue on to her son's place, where she was spending the night. Later Robyn told me that she offered to drive Rhiannon because Marty was creeping her out and she didn't want to be left alone with him.

After Robyn and Rhiannon left, Marty went into a tirade; he was frustrated by having to have a late dinner, and then Robyn left so early. I guess he thought she'd been a bit rude and ungrateful.

Marty and I argued until I'd had enough and decided to leave. As Marty had picked me up, I didn't have my car and had to walk home. Fortunately I only lived a couple of streets away. When I got to a roundabout down the street, Marty appeared in his car. He was speeding down the road, driving erratically, then went flying over the roundabout and straight towards me. I just managed to jump out of the way before he hit me. And all the while he was leaning out of the window screaming at me to get me into the car. I was so glad to get home and locked the door immediately.

The next day, Marty was full of apologies. He pleaded with me to talk to him, to go out for coffee, and eventually I agreed. Although the previous night's incident had rattled me, I thought it was just a one-off and something entirely out of character for Marty. And I could

Cathie's beautiful birthday gift

understand how he might have been frustrated by Robyn's lateness. So I accepted his apology and forgot about the whole incident.

For my birthday in late November, we went to the Winelarder. Marty had brought two cakes for me, and one had my name on it. We were having a lovely time until my friend Mark gave me a birthday kiss—on the lips. This sent Marty into a meltdown, to which Mark replied, 'I'm gay, mate.' It should have been a simple misunderstanding that we all laughed about, but the mood took such a bad turn that we left.

Afterwards we went back to Cathie's, where she presented me with a large artwork she had painted for my birthday. It was just stunning. She had painted another one, but wasn't happy with it and had left it in her garage. I persuaded her to let me see the 'reject' painting, and took a photo of it and had it put onto canvas so I could have two beautiful paintings by Cathie.

Everyone should have been delighted with Cathie's beautiful gift—I certainly was—but it had a strange effect on Marty. He carefully helped me get it home, but he felt a bit down because he thought Cathie's gift was better than anything he had done for my birthday. Marty knew how honoured I was that Cath had done two paintings for me. I had told her I loved her to bits, was very proud to call her my best friend and that my feelings would never change. Perhaps Marty felt jealous. He was certainly in a strange mood.

Everything came to a head on Boxing Day. My son, Sam, and his girlfriend, Tahlia, were going home to Mooroopna after spending Christmas with us. Marty drove us all to Broadmeadows station so they could catch the train. I got out of the car and started walking up to the station with Sam and Tahlia, but then I realised Marty wasn't with us; he was still standing beside his car. I went back and asked what was wrong, and he said he was upset and angry because I had walked off and not worried about him. I had just assumed Marty would walk up to the station with us and didn't think he needed to be invited. It was the most innocent and inconsequential act, but Marty cracked it. He stood by his car, absolutely

A good Samaritan helping change my
tyre, with Cathie providing moral support

fuming, furious that we hadn't held hands and walked
with the kids to the station.

The car ride home was horrific. We both sat there in
stony silence until Marty pulled up at my house, when
I told him I wanted nothing more to do with him. I said
that if he couldn't understand I was saying goodbye to
my son—a son I didn't see that much—and that he was
only worried about himself, then I had no time for him.
No one comes between me and my children.

I BEGAN 2015 as a freshly single woman and saw in the
new year with a bunch of girlfriends. We took a road trip
down to Barwon Heads, where we saw Daryl Braithwaite.
It was a lovely way to bring in 2015, with good food, good

wine, great friends, and not a care in the world. Marty Norman was well and truly in my rear-view mirror. Or so I thought.

Early in January—on what was my daughter Amity's birthday—Cathie and I went to Elwood Food & Wine to see our friend Fabian perform. We had popped outside so Cathie could have a cigarette—she was still smoking in those days—and who should walk around the corner but Marty? I was surprised to see him there—Elwood is a long way from his home in Craigieburn. He came to say hello and after some small talk, Cathie invited him in to join us.

Back inside, I went to the ladies' room with Cathie; I had some questions for her. I wanted to know why she had asked Marty to join us when she knew I had broken up with him and didn't want to see him again. She said she thought I had over-reacted and was too harsh on Marty, and that I should give him another go. Back in November he had found a gas leak at her house, and ever since then she thought he was wonderful. And she wasn't the only one who thought I had been too harsh. My sister, Michelle, thought so too. I didn't make up my mind there and then, but after going home to think things over, I decided to give Marty a second chance.

If I'd known what was happening at our table while Cathie and I were in the ladies' room, I might not have agreed to give Marty another chance. Some time later Fabian told me that he and Marty had a weird conversation, which included Marty asking why I took my phone to the ladies' room and why I hadn't left it on the table. Why was my phone any of his business?

Our evening out, which had started on a high note, ended on a low one when I discovered to my dismay that

I had a flat tyre. I stopped at a service station and tried to put air in it, to no avail. Fortunately a kind gentleman who was also pumping up his tyres put the spare on for me. There *are* good, kind people in this world!

IN FEBRUARY Marty and I were back together. He started coming to a lot of gigs around town with me and my friends. I've always been into the music scene and knew a lot of the artists we went to see. We saw my friends John Swan and Jimmy Cupples at Musicland. We had an enjoyable time catching up, and John serenaded me with the song 'Lady, What's Your Name?'. We also went to see Daryl Braithwaite again at Doncaster Shopping-town Hotel. Marty got up to dance with us and we all had a great time. Afterwards we went to The Flying Saucer, a live music club in Elsternwick. And that's when things started getting weird again.

Marty dropped us off and then said he was going to visit a friend, but shortly afterwards we saw him wander-ing around outside. Eventually he came back in and saw the end of the show, and I don't think he'd been to see his friend or ever intended to. At the time, with a couple of drinks in me, I just dismissed this strange incident, but in retrospect it was probably a red flag.

Around this time, my car developed an oil leak. Then one day in March I was reversing out of the driveway and found the steering wheel wouldn't turn. I had to leave the car at home and walk to work. When Marty came in for morning tea that day I told him what had happened. He seemed to know exactly what was wrong with my car; it was the power steering. He asked for my keys and said he would go over to my place and try to fix the car, but if he couldn't he'd take it to his mechanic. He ended up taking my car to the mechanic, then came back to work and drove me home after I finished my shift. I thought he was being kind and generous.

With my car fixed, I was able to help Rhiannon get some driving experience on her newly acquired learner permit. So at Easter Marty organised for us to go down to Rosebud to visit his mother. We picked up Marty's daughter from her apartment in Richmond, and off we went. I would like to say it was a lovely day, but alas, it wasn't. Marty and his sister did not get along and had a huge argument. His sister stormed off and went out the back to the flat she lived in, and we left.

We went down to Rosebud again on Anzac Day to march in the parade. Marty was hoping to wear his father's medals, but as his nephew usually wears the medals this sparked another argument with his sister. Marty ended up wearing the medals, but then his niece accused him of pushing her children out of the way so he could hold his mother's hand during the parade. I defended Marty; I didn't see him push anyone and didn't believe he did. We ended up having a very tumultuous lunch at the RSL in Rosebud, and I couldn't wait to leave. The whole day was full of tension.

Later, in the car, Marty made the startling confession that he *had* pushed his niece's children. I was disgusted to realise I had defended him when all the time his family were telling me the truth.

On the way home Marty wanted to stop at Sexyland—an 'adult' store. I didn't—it's not my thing—and I was tired. He said okay, but then ignored my wishes, turned off the freeway and went to the store anyway. I stayed in the car, but he was taking forever so I went inside and looked at the clothes and boots that were on sale.

Everyone knows I love my boots! Once I'd had enough I told Marty that I wanted to go. He wouldn't leave until I chose a movie, so I just pointed at one so we could get out of there. It wasn't like I was going to watch it.

There were other odd little things that happened during this period. Once we were driving through Mickleham and Marty slowed down and pointed out a house where a woman was attacked and killed by her adulterous husband and his mistress. Years later, the husband hanged himself in the garage. Why was Marty so keen to show me this house? We watched a lot of movies together, and I remember being freaked out by the movie *Sleeping with the Enemy* with Julia Roberts. I was on the edge of my seat while we watched it, a fact that Marty found funny. But I didn't see anything funny about fear.

During our relationship, Marty and I spent our time together at his house. My daughter, and sometimes her boyfriend, were at my house, and I didn't want Marty's presence to make them feel uncomfortable. I also wanted to get to know Marty better before I put my full trust in him. I had a teenage daughter, and it was natural for me to feel this way. But I had also noticed that Marty didn't have a great relationship with his own children.

Marty told me there had been some kind of accident with his son, some sort of physical injury, and his son blamed Marty for it and wanted nothing more to do with his father. Marty's youngest daughter lived in another state and he never saw her. His eldest daughter was the only one who would have anything to do with him, and it had to be on her terms. He would call and call, and eventually she would call him back and have a brief conversation. His eldest daughter had also blocked him on Facebook.

Given his poor relationship with his own children, I didn't appreciate it when Marty tried to discipline Rhiannon about her boyfriend one day—this was not on and I immediately became angry. I raised my voice to Marty and told him that he wasn't Rhiannon's father and he needed to butt out. He needed to let me discipline my own daughter, and learn his place in my life and that my children are just that—*my* children. He had no right to interfere with my parenting and it was his problem, not mine, if he didn't like that. Marty was not happy. He started fuming and sulking, then stormed out of my house.

Things began to go from bad to worse after this. The impeccably dressed man I had met a few months ago, who never had a hair out of place, was now wearing the same Holden branded shirt and tracksuit pants every day. I found it embarrassing to be with someone who dressed like that and asked him not to, but he ignored me.

Marty also insisted on driving me everywhere. At first I thought it was sweet; his helpfulness and attentiveness freed up headspace that let me deal with my elderly mother more easily. With Marty driving, I didn't have to worry about getting Mum in and out of the car and things like that. He even took Mum's car to be detailed and got all the cobwebs out of it. But it got to the point where I couldn't go anywhere without him—not to gigs with my girlfriends or over to Cathie's or anywhere. Before I began dating Marty I'd always been out and about with Cathie and other friends. Now, I was either at work or with Marty. Cathie was calling and messaging and asking me to come over, or to go with her here or there, but I kept saying no. Cathie was wondering where I fitted in her life. I had become one of those people who don't see their friends any more when they have a new boyfriend. But I wasn't that person; Cathie was still very important to me.

Marty had gradually become more and more controlling without me even noticing. This behaviour had slowly crept up on me, and now I seemed to have little time for anyone else in my life. Things came to a head when I had to take my mother to an appointment with the surgeon who was going to do her knee replacement. On the day of her appointment, Marty's mother was arriving from Rosebud to visit him. We were in the car, coming back from shopping or maybe dinner, and Marty told me what was going to happen when his mother visited. He said I was to go with him to Craigieburn station and wait for his mother to arrive, then we would go and pick up my mother, and all four us would go to the surgeon's appointment. Not only did I object to having my time mapped out like this, the idea of his mother—a woman my mother had never met—coming to something as private as a surgeon's appointment was ludicrous.

I was at the end of my tether with Marty's behaviour and this pushed me over the edge. I told him off. I said I couldn't take any more of his controlling nature, that I was a grown up and could look after myself, and that I didn't need him to oversee everything in my life. I insisted that whatever this relationship was, it was over. I was done. I demanded that he take me home, and again said that we were through. I wanted nothing more to do with him.

CHAPTER 2

THE NIGHTMARE BEGINS

I WAS very upset by the whole experience I'd had with Marty over the business with his mother, and didn't go into work the next day. At lunchtime, I went over to Cathie's; I needed some girl-talk. While we were talking there was a knock at the back door. Cathie's front door was jammed shut due to the timber warping, so friends always came to the back door. Cathie said, 'You answer it, it's probably for you.' She was right. I opened the door and Marty was standing there. He said he'd called into Big W looking for me, but was told I was off sick. He said he had been to my house, then my doctor's, and then to Cathie's trying to find me. He began pleading with me to take him back, to give him another chance.

I was angry that he'd been traipsing around the place looking for me after I had told him in no uncertain terms that I never wanted to see him again. 'Who does that?' I asked him. 'No one does, and even if you did go to all these places looking for me, why tell me? It's just embarrassing.' I told him to go, to leave me alone. Then he left and went home, or so I thought...

By the time we got Marty out of the house it was about five o'clock. His visit had really rattled me and I thought a glass of wine would help me calm down, so we walked up to the Winelarder. We bought our drinks at the bar, turned around, and there was Marty. Again he began pleading with me to take him back. Again I told him to leave. He became angry, yelling and swearing at me, demanding that I take him back. The shouting went on and on. Marty was scaring the other patrons and the owners said they would call the police if I didn't make him leave, but he wasn't listening to me. Cathie and I went outside in an effort to get Marty to leave, but he continued to make a scene. Desperate, I called his eldest daughter and asked for help. She called Marty, told him to leave, then rang me back to say he was going. I had never been so glad to see the back of someone.

But this was only the beginning of the nightmare.

Marty began contacting my friends and pleading with them to talk me into taking him back. I didn't like the fact that he was calling my friends and was even more disturbed that he seemed to know where I was all the time. Although he claimed to have been to my work looking for me the day after we broke up, I knew my colleagues would never tell anyone where I was.

I called the local police station in Craigieburn to ask if they could search my phone and car for tracking devices, but they said they couldn't. Instead, they advised me to go to court to obtain an intervention order. I was disappointed; I thought the police were there to help me.

The policeman I spoke to told me to message Marty and tell him I had sought police help. This is what I sent him...

Today I went into the Police Station for advice in regard to you...since you're not leaving me alone...turning up no matter where I am...messaging me and my friends...I have told them everything and the policeman told me to contact Broadmeadows Court and to get an intervention order on you...the policeman himself is very worried about me as you are not listening to me when I'm asking you to leave me alone...I don't want to hear or see you ever again...I have made this perfectly clear...again I am asking you to please leave me alone...

This was Marty's reply...

I will leave you alone, just so shattered that this has happened when we had so much love for each other...Been trying to reach out to people to understand why you are making me out to be such a horrible person. Don't know why this reaction with every-thing I did for you and I only have your best interests, health and happiness at heart. Why tell people I'm a bad person? You are everything to me Di, please don't throw our love away. I am so shattered and feel so empty and sick. Please don't go to Court or the Police, this would be so hurtful as I only care for you Di...
I will leave you alone.

I found this reply over the top, as we had never been that serious. But the last few words gave me some relief, and I was hopeful that I wouldn't have to take things any further with the authorities. The idea of applying for an intervention order was quite overwhelming. I knew nothing about the law or the courts and found the idea of going down this track very stressful.

A WEEK LATER I went to my cousin's sixtieth birthday party in Berwick. I was really looking forward to letting my hair down and having a happy, relaxing time now that

I had Marty off my back. The theme for the party was the 1970s and I got myself kitted up in my best Stevie Nicks outfit, complete with top hat. I wanted to show my cool outfit to Cathie, so I went round to the Winelarder on my way to the party, thinking she'd be there. She wasn't, but I saw my old boyfriend was having a drink at the bar. I joined him and had a coffee before I set off to the party.

The party was well underway when I arrived, and it was great to catch up with the relatives and friends who had come from far and wide to celebrate my cousin's milestone birthday. But not long after I arrived, the mood turned sour. One of the guests came in and exclaimed that the tyres on all our cars had been slashed. I couldn't believe it. Everybody was stunned. The police were called and we took turns talking to them. Many people had had two of their tyres slashed, so they couldn't just put on the spare to go home. Talk about killing the mood.

I was one of the people who'd had two tyres slashed. I called a close childhood friend, Trevor, who is like a brother to me. In fact my children call him 'Uncle Trevor'. He's also a tow truck driver and had the tyres I needed, so he kindly came over to replace my slashed tyres so I could drive home.

When I went into Beaurepaires to have my tyres replaced I told them what had happened, and they gave me a huge discount, which I appreciated. At that time we were thinking it was kids who'd attacked all the cars, but these days I'm not so sure. Had Marty been following me that night? Did he see me with my ex at the Winelarder? Did that send him into a blind rage that led him to lash out at all the cars parked near mine? This is speculation—just my opinion—but in light of future events, I believe that's what happened.

Given that Marty had admitted to going around to my house to look for me, I thought I should talk to my neighbour about what was going on. After visiting Mum on Mother's Day, I went home and told my neighbour, Penny, that Marty and I had broken up. I asked her to please let me know if she saw him there. I was astonished when Penny told me that Marty was there all the time, and that he was letting himself in with a key. How did he get a key? I had never given him one! It must have been the day I gave him my keys so he could fix the steering problem with my car. At the time I thought he was being kind; now it looked like he was taking advantage of a situation to get himself a copy of my house key. Penny had also noticed that when Marty 'visited' my house he looked around to see who was watching, and she was worried that Marty was coming around when Rhiannon was at home. Penny also said this had been going on for a while. Just when I was optimistic about getting Marty out of my life, I was discovering how deeply embedded he had become.

I rang a locksmith first thing Monday morning. He said he could be at my house at 1:00 pm, so I changed my lunchbreak to be there. While the locksmith was changing my locks, who should turn up but Marty? He just walked straight through the open front door without bothering to knock. I asked him how he knew I was at home, and he said my staff had told him. I yelled at him to leave. He yelled back at me and demanded I return the Fleetwood Mac tickets he had purchased for us before we broke up. The shouting was so loud the locksmith, who was outside in his van, heard us and was about to call the police. Then Marty abruptly left. After the locksmith finished up we had a bit of a chat, and he offered to be a witness should I need one for the police. I was touched by the kindness of this stranger.

But this incident wasn't over. After the locksmith left, I opened the door to leave the house and found Marty standing there. I tried to shut the door, but he pushed it open further and Roxy, my new puppy, snuck out. I pushed past Marty, slammed the door shut behind me and went chasing after my dog.

When I got back to work, I asked everyone if they had told Marty where I was. They said they hadn't seen him at all. So how did he know I was at home? Could he have somehow put a tracker on my car or on my phone? Did that explain his strange comment to Fabian about me not leaving my phone on the table at the Winelarder? I thought back to the day after we broke up and Marty came round to Cathie's, telling me he'd called into my work, and been to my house and my doctor's looking for me. Were those lies to put me off the scent?

I started looking through my phone. After searching for what seemed like hours, I found some very odd things in the location settings, which showed that my phone had been accessed remotely. I sent a screen shot to Rhiannon, which showed that my phone was accessed three times during the morning while I was at work. It showed two points—where my phone was and where the other person's phone was at the time the remote access took place. When I zoomed in, I realised it was near Marty's home. And then I found a few other times my phone had been accessed.

I told Rhiannon about this and she told me off for not doing any of the updates Apple sent me. Then she installed the updates, which would take out any bugs in my phone, and also did a factory reset before reinstating all my data and files.

I hoped that whatever tracker may have been on my phone was gone, but I couldn't be sure so I called the police in Craigieburn and asked again if they had a device that could check my phone and car for a tracker. They didn't; however, they did advise me again to get an intervention order on Marty. I was hoping it wouldn't come to this. The thought of applying for an intervention order was confronting and overwhelming. I was busy looking after my elderly mother and a teenage daughter who was having trouble at school. I had a job that kept me busy. I knew nothing about the court system and knew no one who could help me with this.

Later that month, on 26 May, there was a knock on my door. When I looked through the peephole I saw Marty standing on my doorstep. I didn't answer and called the police again, but was told that without an intervention order there was not much they could do to help me.

Marty then turned up at Craigieburn Central one day. I was on my way to Gloria Jeans for lunch, and when I saw Marty I just kept walking and told him to leave. I sat down at a table in the restaurant, and Marty sat down as well, once again pleading with me to take him back. Eventually he left, but then came back with a letter for me. The contents were the usual sickly-sweet nonsense about how sorry he was and how much he loved me and how special I was to him and how could I break his heart like that. Blah, blah, blah... I wasn't fooled. This was self-indulgent emotional drivel all about his pain, and I ignored it.

But all the while Marty had been at Gloria Jeans I was thinking, *my phone, my phone*, which was on the table. Was he trying to get close enough to put the tracker back on it? When I checked later, my fears were justified—the tracker was back on my phone. I had turned the location settings off, but this obviously hadn't helped. Rhiannon tried to get the tracker off again and unfortunately I lost text messages from Marty, which I could have used as evidence in the legal proceedings to come.

I was really starting to fear for my safety. Paranoia was setting in and the tracker on my phone was really freaking me out. I needed my phone; I couldn't just get rid of it, but If I had it with me I was pretty sure Marty would know where I was.

And then my car was attacked again. My friend Mandy was coming down from Benalla, and she and Cathie and I were having a night out. We left my car at Cathie's place and went to the Winelarder for a drink before heading out to Brunswick to see Jon Stevens perform. When we got into my car, we found the passenger-side mirror had been smashed. The passenger window also had gouges in it, indicating that someone had tried to smash the window as well. This wasn't the only time attacks happened while I was at Cathie's place. It was so unfair that she was getting caught up in these attacks just because she was my friend. She had never had a relationship with Marty; she was an innocent bystander.

This was getting crazy. I had to find some way to protect myself.

The next day I went into a Telstra shop to see the technician and hopefully get the tracker off my phone. He made an adjustment to the phone and the tracker came off, but when I asked him to go back in and double-check to make sure the tracker was gone he discovered it was still there. The poor guy kept trying, but eventually threw his arms up in the air and said it was beyond him to fix. He advised getting a replacement phone and new phone number. I left feeling frustrated, as I would have to pay to cancel my contract with the telco. My 'brother' Trevor had told me to keep the phone in foil to block all signals; I don't know how true this is, but I was desperate enough to try it.

I was so over my life... I decided it was time for me to take legal action and apply through the courts for an intervention order, using my phone as evidence.

ON 4 JUNE 2015, I went into Broadmeadows Magistrates Court to find out how to get an intervention order. After giving me some forms to fill out, the staff checked them over and told me to take a seat. I was lucky; it was a quiet afternoon and a magistrate would be able to see me that day. In all the times I went to court in this whole sorry saga, this was the only time I wasn't kept waiting! After I was called in and presented my case and evidence, I was given an interim intervention order that would last for a month. In July I would go to court and hopefully be granted a full intervention order. Meanwhile, Marty would be served with the interim order, which would give me some protection.

The intervention order, or IVO, had the usual conditions. These conditions required Marty to stay away from me physically, but also stated that he must not look for me, follow me, keep me under surveillance, intentionally damage my property, publish material about me on the internet or even attempt to contact me or communicate with me. If he wanted to talk to me, it would have to be through a lawyer. With these conditions in place, I felt relieved and did believe that the harassment and stalking would soon stop and I would have my life back. Sadly, I was wrong.

Soon after I got the interim IVO on Marty, I had a call from the owners of the Winelarder. Someone had sent them a 'nasty' letter about me. I went over to pick it up and was completely devastated when I read the contents. The letter was supposedly from a 'patron' of the bar who claimed to work at the 'Vice Squad' as a 'Private Investigator'. This patron claimed to have been observing me, and said that he found my antics at the bar offensive. He stated that my behaviour was promiscuous and bordered on prostitution. He also called me a 'working class old tart', who had 'more pricks in her than a dartboard'. Most shocking of all—he used my full name.

The contents of this letter were utterly shocking, and there was something else about it that almost made my heart stop—it used the same kind of formatting as the letter Marty had given me at Gloria Jeans the previous Friday. The tabbing for the paragraphs was eerily similar. He must have written it. I was devastated that he could say these things about me. And why? Why would he want to hurt me?

If it hadn't been so hurtful, I might have laughed at the letter Marty left at the Winelarder. Didn't he know there is no such thing as the 'Vice Squad' in Australia? Who did he think he was? Don Johnson from Miami Vice? I could at least be grateful that my friends at the Winelarder didn't believe the letter was in any way genuine. They could have just thrown the letter away, but gave it to me so I could use it as evidence. It was nice to know my friends were looking out for me.

By now it had been quite a while since I had broken up with Marty, but one day one of the girls from centre management at Craigieburn Central came to see me. She told me Marty had been talking to them about me. He seemed to know all about my personal problems, and the information he was giving them was so detailed it made her think he was stalking me. He was telling them where

I was going and who I was seeing, and all about the problems breaking up with me had caused him. Marty wanted to be seen as a victim, and it seemed he was succeeding. Centre management were quite annoyed by his visits and wanted me to stop Marty from going to see them. My boss, Pauline, emailed Big W head office to tell them what was going on and gave me a copy of the email to take to court.

This business with Marty was becoming very stressful, but I tried to carry on with my life. Rhiannon and I are mad Hawthorn supporters, so we went to the footy at the MCG to see Hawthorn vs. Sydney. We had boundary seats near the goals and it was a fantastic day. It felt great not to think about Marty and all the trouble he was causing me for a few hours. I had parked my car at Craigieburn station and we took the train in, but when we got back to the station and started driving home something about my tyres felt strange. I stopped to check them, but it was after 8 pm and in the dark I couldn't find anything wrong. I drove to the service station and checked the air, and it was fine. But as we kept going the car started vibrating so much I thought the tyre or something was going to come through the floor. I could have called the RACV, but it was late and wet, we didn't have far to drive and we just wanted to get home. The vibrations were so intense that we were scared we'd have a major accident. I drove home at a crawl; both Rhiannon and I were terrified.

This incident occurred on the Queen's Birthday long weekend, and my sister Michelle and her husband, Rob, were coming over for a visit. I asked Robbie to take my car for a drive, but after just a few metres he had to pull over. He checked my tyres and pulled a set of spikes from the driver's side front tyre. I said the passenger-side seemed worse, and Rob found another row of spikes on that tyre. These weren't a couple of stray nails or screws that had got stuck in my tyres as I drove over them—the spikes were perfectly and carefully attached to the tyres. Rob's a mechanic, and he believed the spikes had been deliberately attached. In fact, he said they were probably hammered onto my tyres. I rang the train station to ask about looking at CCTV footage, but they needed the police to obtain it for me. I rang Craigieburn Police Station, but no one answered. Both fear and frustration began to build in me.

When the police didn't answer their phone, I went to the station in person and filled out a report with Sergeant Williams. He said he would ring the train station and hopefully obtain the CCTV footage. Then I went to JB Hi-Fi and bought a dash cam, spending the first few of many thousands of dollars I would spend on security measures to protect myself.

I wasn't the only one feeling frightened, frustrated and angry. This situation was affecting my family and friends. By this stage, Rhiannon was very angry with me. She was sick of all the drama going on and called her dad for help. He apparently called Marty, who told him I was taking cocaine and other nonsense. He claimed he had broken up with me because I was taking drugs?! WTF!!! I was concerned that such allegations might affect my custody of Rhiannon, so I went to the trouble and expense of taking a drug test. Needless to say the results were negative.

Nobody believed these wild accusations, but nevertheless my ex and my daughter were frustrated and angry about the intrusions Marty was making in their lives. They didn't want to know about him or my problems with him. It was so hard to make people understand that I was utterly powerless over his actions, and that I had done nothing to set him on this crazy path.

Now I had my family yelling at me for all the horrible things that were happening, but I didn't know why they were happening and had failed again and again to stop the madness. Rhiannon was terrified for her life when she was in my car, and so scared and anxious that she didn't want to be around me—my very presence terrified my daughter. After the incident with the spikes on my tyres, she fled to her boyfriend's place and left me on my own. It was beyond heartbreaking. My ex-husband was furious, but unwilling to get involved. I had to sort it out on my own, but I was failing. Even Cathie—my best friend—was screaming at me to make it all go away. She was sick of becoming involved when Marty attacked while I was at her place. But I couldn't make it go away, and I hadn't asked for any of this. All I did was accept an invitation for coffee, and a few months later my life had descended into a never-ending nightmare that was getting worse by the day.

I had no support, no help, and was alone with my fear and failure. I was beside myself. In my head, I had no one. Would they care if I was here? Probably not. Rhiannon hadn't been home for days. Amity was living in Queensland. Cathie was sick of hearing about what Marty was doing to me and didn't want to talk to me. No one had called to check on me since the incident with my tyres. I'd heard nothing from my friends and family. I felt completely alone, out of my depth with the chaos that was now my life. What could I possibly do to make this all go away...

I went to the bathroom and opened the medicine cabinet.

CHAPTER 3

DESCENT INTO MADNESS

WHEN I WOKE up on 15 June 2015, I couldn't believe I was still alive. I had been convinced that all those pills would end the nightmare. I thought, *That'd be right, I can't even kill myself properly.* I called in sick for work, feeling like a worthless piece of crap. I was nauseated, and vomited and vomited, but had no one to call. Everybody was angry and over it—over me talking about it. I felt like I had no one. Probably I should have gone to hospital, but I stayed home and dealt with the fallout of my suicide attempt. Dark, lonely days followed...

I stayed home alone for three days. And those three days gave me time to think; I searched my soul and decided I needed to fight. I needed to fight for my life, my family, my friends. I thought, *This is going to stop. I'll get the full intervention order; I'll then have police help and Marty will finally leave me alone. I'll have the law on my side, I'll be safe.* My thoughts had flipped. I believed I had survived for a reason. What I didn't know was how long and brutal that fight would be.

CATHIE HAD BEEN away on the weekend I attempted suicide, but she was due back in Melbourne the following weekend and would be expecting to see me. She was my best friend, and I had to tell her what I'd tried to do. After that, she messaged me every day asking, '*Are you still alive!!!*' She'd worry if she hadn't heard from me. It might sound like a confronting thing to ask someone who had attempted suicide, but that was Cathie. She called a spade a spade and I knew that asking this question was an expression of love.

By the following Saturday, 20 June, I was feeling well enough to go out and start living my life again. I went to the Winelarder to see a friend perform, then afterwards I went back to Cathie's. Her partner had cooked up a lovely supper of beef and Asian salad. Before I left, at around 11 pm, Cathie and I checked my car—something we had started doing as a matter of course. It might sound like paranoia, but it was justified paranoia. Sure enough, we found damage to the driver's side windscreen wiper and aerial, and my mirror had been broken.

We rang Triple Zero and Senior Constable Adam Williamson from Bayside Police Station rang me back about half an hour later. We spoke for a while, but then he recommended we hang up because he didn't trust my phone. I gave him Cathie's number and he called back on her phone. Police arrived at 12:30 am to take photos and record some details. They also took the SD (Secure Digital) card from my dashcam to give to Senior Constable Williamson. I didn't get home until after 2 am.

The next day Rhiannon and I went to a Telstra store to buy a new phone and get a new phone number for me. I left my current phone at home, hoping that Marty would think I was there. The phone number Marty had for me was now disconnected, and Cathie had given my new phone number to Adam Williamson. She was hopeful that he would help me. She said '*I really want to catch Marty!!! I really think he is very dangerous!!!*' I hoped having a new phone would give me some peace of mind, but I didn't think the nightmare was over. And I was right.

On Monday morning, one of the managers at work came in from her lunchbreak and told me Marty had been walking around the carpark talking to himself. When he came across my car, he left; it was obvious that's what he'd been looking for. Now that I had a new phone, he couldn't track me and actually had to come looking for my car. I was relieved that he hadn't tried to inflict more damage on my car, but I called both Bayside and Craigieburn Police Stations. This is when I discovered Marty hadn't yet been served with the interim intervention order because the courts hadn't sent through the paperwork. No wonder he was still hanging around. I was absolutely furious and my frustration with the 'system' was growing. Fortunately, Raelene Conway from Craigieburn Police Station did her best to help and got in touch with the Magistrates Court to sort things out. Marty was served that evening.

I hoped that having Marty served would calm things down, but no. On the following Saturday, I went over to Cathie's to celebrate her birthday. We went to the Winelarder for a couple of drinks, then back to Cathie's for dinner. When we got to her place we saw that my car had been egged. The petrol door was also open and the petrol cap was gone. Interfering with my car was clearly a breach of the interim intervention order, but how could I prove it was Marty who had done this?

On the way home I rang Craigieburn Police Station to tell them what had happened. We were worried about what might be in my petrol tank, so the policeman stayed on the phone with me for part of the journey home. God forbid I have an accident and get hurt or killed, or kill someone else. The situation was utterly nerve wracking. I was terrified and drove as slowly as I could over the West Gate Bridge, all the time worried that I could be dead at any moment if my car broke down or somehow caused an accident.

Later Cathie called to say they had found spikes on the road where my car had been parked; apparently, this time they had either fallen off or failed to attach to my tyres. I couldn't believe this had happened again, but thanked God it hadn't worked this time. I was grateful for small mercies.

The next day I took Rhiannon to work in a car with egg all over it, then went to the car wash. I also went into Supercheap Auto to buy new wipers and a lockable petrol cap. My next task was to ring Ford to re-program my remote car access. They talked me through what to do over the phone, and said this would cancel any other remotes that could open my car. I also printed out photos of my car's damage to take to the court hearing that was scheduled for a couple of days later. I was so frustrated at all the trouble I had to go to and all the time it took just to be able to drive around and feel safe—like I had before Marty started messing up my life.

The court date for the intervention order couldn't come fast enough.

THE HEARING FOR the intervention order was on 1 July. The day before I was booked in at the Austin Hospital for carpal tunnel surgery, but was so preoccupied dealing with my other troubles that I'd almost forgotten about it. It's stressful enough having surgery, or going to court, and there I was doing both in the space of two days. My hand was very painful after the surgery, but I couldn't let that stop me from going to court. I had to put an end to Marty's harassment. I needed that restraining order to survive.

On 1 July 2015, I went to Broadmeadows Magistrates Court for the hearing on my intervention order application. I arrived thinking the police would be helping me, given that the IVO had been their suggestion. But I was utterly naïve. To my dismay I discovered the police would not be helping me. Instead, I was told to go and see the duty lawyer. When I spoke to the lawyer, I was devastated to be told they were unable to help me as they had a conflict—they had had previous dealings with Marty and would be defending him. I was sent downstairs to Legal Aid, and after waiting for hours and hours to see them I was told that they couldn't help me either. I was the Applicant; they could only help the Respondent.[1] So why in heaven's name did the duty lawyer tell me to see them?

There I was, recovering from a suicide attempt, still feeling the effects of the previous day's surgery and dealing with a crazy stalker, only to find I would have to go court for the first time in my life and represent myself after having done no preparation. I was upset, angry and over everything.

When I finally got into the courtroom, I was relieved that the magistrate seemed very understanding, and I told him everything that had been going on. Magistrate Bentley wanted to see the letter the Winelarder had

---

1   This situation had changed at the time of writing. Legal Aid is now able to represent both Applicant and Respondent.

received, and also wanted Marty's lawyer to see it. After reading the letter the lawyer claimed that anyone could have written it. But Magistrate Bentley told Marty to not insult his intelligence, that he knew he had written it, and by looking at me he could tell I didn't have any enemies. I wasn't surprised to hear this. It was obvious that Marty had written the letter.

Marty's lawyer then tried to persuade me to take Marty's offer of an 'Undertaking'. This is an option that the Respondent in an intervention order application can pursue, and is a written promise to the court to agree to certain conditions—in this case, the conditions were to leave me alone. However, if there's a breach of the promise, there is no criminal conviction—unlike when an IVO is breached. This means that an undertaking is not as protective as an intervention order. I didn't know this at the time, and felt uncomfortable having to make a decision about something I was poorly informed about.

But what I did know was that Marty's word meant nothing; he'd promised to leave me alone before and broken that promise repeatedly. I refused to accept the undertaking. After that, the magistrate referred to the letter and said it was full of hatred. He urged Marty to save us all a lot of time and agree to the order. Then we broke for lunch.

My aunt had come to support me that day, and we went across the street to a Degani's cafe for lunch. And can you believe it—Marty saw us sitting inside and came in. So much for his promise to leave me alone.

The intervention order application listed various details, including the places that would be off limits to Marty. When we resumed after lunch, Marty's lawyer asked me to take my workplace off the order so that Marty could still shop there. She stated that he would have to stay five metres away from me. I saw problems with this, as the checkout was in the area of the store where I worked supervising the front end. I asked how Marty would pay for any purchases. The lawyer said, 'We'll let the magistrate decide then.' Magistrate Bentley said Marty would have to shop at another Big W and that he would be refused entry to Big W Craigieburn for the next twelve months.

I'd successfully represented myself at my first court appearance, and Marty was now legally required to stay at least 200 metres away from my house and Rhiannon's school, stay at least five metres away from me and Rhiannon in any other public place, and not enter my workplace. I felt like I was fulfilling the vow to myself to fight Marty that I made after my suicide attempt. I was sure it would get better from here. Sadly, I didn't know in that moment how wrong I was. I didn't know that everything would get so much worse before it got better.

IT WASN'T LONG before I felt Marty's unwelcome presence in my life again. On 12 July, I opened the front door to leave home and found a used condom on my doormat. Rhiannon and I had been to dinner and a movie the night before and got home close to midnight. If the condom had been there, we'd have seen it, which meant that Marty was now creeping around my house in the middle of the night. The very thought made my skin crawl.

The next day Marty came to Big W and stood outside in the rain, watching me work through the windows. I didn't see him, but one of my co-workers, Sue, told me about it the next day. I organised for Craigieburn police to have the relevant security footage, and later that week Sue and I went to Craigieburn Police Station to give statements.

On the Friday, Sergeant Williams from Craigieburn Police Station picked up Marty for questioning over being outside my workplace, but as my workplace didn't have the 200-metre ruling attached to it he was not charged. Even though I had a full intervention order, I was not as safe as I thought I was going to be. When Sergeant Williams asked Marty why he wouldn't leave me alone, he replied that it was because I loved him. Clearly Marty had no sense of what love is. He was trying to hurt me, and thought that was love. The police told him to stay away from the front of the store, and not go to Gloria Jeans and sit there all day watching me.

The following Monday, 20 July, was the first anniversary of my father's passing. It was a sad day made sadder when Christine from the Winelarder frantically messaged Cathie and me to say that another typed letter had been found on the wine racks. The note was an invitation for men to get me drunk and rape me. There were a lot of tradies working in the area, building new apartments, and I assumed it was meant for them. So, this is the love Marty was talking about... The same day Cathie discovered someone—we assumed it was Marty—had tampered with the mirrors on her car. They had been bent right back and she could see nothing in them. She nearly had an accident after picking up her son from school.

Marty was everywhere. One day I saw him standing outside Aldi at Craigieburn Central, watching me walk to my car. After this 'sighting' I rang the Women's Legal Service for advice, but they were unable to help due to a conflict of interest—apparently they had helped Marty in the past. Really? But he's a man! I thought the service was for women and found this upsetting. The next day I had more luck with the Law Institute, who gave me a list of lawyers who specialise in these type of cases and whose fees I might be able to have compensated through Victims of Crime, the government body that offers free information and support for people affected by crime. I had to find a lawyer I could actually afford!

It had been just three weeks since the intervention order had been granted, and I believed Marty had interfered with me or my friends four times. Obviously I had no proof of this, but I was sure it was him. Who else would it be?

On Friday, 24 July, my friends and I got together for a gig in Oakleigh. I was looking forward to a chance to chill out and forget about Marty for a while. We had a great evening, but when I got back to my car I discovered bright yellow gunk all over it. I couldn't see out the windows and this mystery substance was clumping and dripping from the doors and panels. For safety, I had parked my car at nearby Oakleigh Police Station. I rang the intercom and two police officers came out to look at my car, take photos and look for CCTV cameras that would have captured who did this.

I was with my friend Mandy and we took the car straight to a car wash, but whatever was all over my car didn't come off. After this I was a complete mess and totally lost control of my emotions. Mandy had to drive me home and kindly stayed over at my house that night. The next day I took my car to my friend Darryl, a house painter, who knew instantly what the bright yellow gunk was—insulation foam that expands and hardens when dry. After three hours with a heat gun and scraper, Darryl got most of the stuff off.

Next stop was Craigieburn Central to purchase security cameras. On the way out of Dick Smith, Mandy and I literally ran straight into Marty. I got out my phone and started filming so I could show the police that he was breaking his intervention order. Marty immediately went into a nearby menswear store and for some reason started hassling the manager, who later told me he was trying to get her into the back of the store. She had no idea why he was doing this, and she was scared to death.

Mandy and I then started walking back to my car, but Marty thought we were following and filming him, so he called security. After explaining to the security guard, whom I knew, that we were just walking back to my car, Mandy and I went straight to Craigieburn Police Station. Marty pulled up at the station behind us. Obviously he had followed us there. While we were waiting for police to come to the counter, I spoke directly to Marty. Perhaps this wasn't advisable, but I wanted to remind him about his IVO conditions. I told him he wasn't allowed within five metres of me and had to leave. I was sick of him telling people that I loved him, so I told him that I didn't love him, that I hated him, and that I thought he was a creep.

Police officers came out to the counter and asked what was going on. Marty started screaming at me to 'Do us all a favour and commit suicide.' I couldn't believe how brazen this was. Raelene, a police officer I had spoken to before, asked, 'What did he say?' I said, 'You heard right.' Mandy and I spent the next two and a half hours giving statements. A week later Broadmeadows police called to say that their Domestic Violence Unit would be taking over my case as the file was too much for Craigieburn Police Station to handle.

Marty soon struck again. I was at Elwood Food & Wine Bar, celebrating the birthday of Leeanne, one of the owners. It was hard to relax, as I had become hypervigilant, but after a lot of insistence from Cathie, I eventually got up and headed to the dance floor. Just as I started busting some moves, Leeanne came running in and said my car was 'under attack'. A white Commodore had been driving past and throwing bottles at it. I called the police, and officers from St Kilda Police Station came to take statements. Adding insult to injury, Marty was never charged or spoken to about this incident, as no one had taken photos or written down the number plate of the white Commodore. Everything seemed to be going Marty's way.

One bright note, I thought, was that I would have footage of the incident. Alas, when I checked my car I found the dashcam neatly folded up on the driver's seat. It was then I realised Marty had keys to my car. Reprogramming the remote had been a waste of time. I couldn't seem to stay one step ahead of Marty. I would have to get the locks on my car changed and now it had panel damage—yet more items in the growing list of things wrong with my car.

AFTER BEING GRANTED the intervention order, I had bought a new phone and changed my number, which meant that Marty couldn't trace me that way, but what about my house? I knew Marty had been going inside my house without permission—my neighbour had confirmed that. What bugs or cameras were in there? I was worried that he was watching and listening all the time. I could get a new phone, but I couldn't just get a new house. My friend Mandy and her husband, Michael, came over and installed the security cameras I had purchased.

And what if Marty tampered with my car again? I was scared to go out because I was worried that my car was unsafe, but if I didn't go out, then he was controlling me... damned if I do, damned if I don't. I called the locksmith to change the locks and keys for my car.

And what if Marty hurt my children? What if he found a way to kill me? I contacted the lawyer who had handled my divorce to put my affairs in order. I wanted my children set up so they didn't have to worry about money or where they were going to live should anything happen to me. I felt more at ease after sorting out my affairs, but the lawyer was amused that I wrote my letter to her by hand—I didn't trust my computer.

The list of 'what ifs' was endless and my mind was racing and taking me to dark places. In four short months Marty Norman had turned my life into a living hell. And just when I thought it couldn't get any worse, it did.

Raelene Conway from Craigieburn Police Station called to advise that I was due in court on 20 August, as Marty had applied for an intervention order against me. I was gobsmacked. The basis for the order was that I had filmed Marty when I ran into him outside the menswear store at Craigieburn Central.

I decided to go and talk to the staff at the store about what had happened—it was a good thing I worked at the centre and knew a lot of the employees. I asked the manager, Mimi, at the menswear store if she would write something for me to take to court, which she kindly agreed to do. She also told me Marty came in the day after the filming 'incident' and spent forty-five minutes verbally abusing the staff. He told the poor salesgirl she was useless, gave lousy service and was a whore. Charming... Mimi had called security, who escorted Marty out of the building. In trying to explain his outburst to the security staff, Marty had told them he was missing his wife. What wife? Did he mean me? Could this get any crazier?

The day after my son Sam's birthday, Raelene Conway came into the store to serve me with an order to appear in court for Marty's IVO application against me. I took this opportunity to build my own case against Marty. I showed her the damage to my car that had been inflicted the previous weekend. We went to the menswear store where Marty had retreated the day I filmed him and the staff gave Raelene details about his behaviour. Police from Broadmeadows followed this up with photographs of my car and official statements. They also said they would apply to the court to include the whole of Craigieburn Central, not just Big W, on my order. Just as Marty was seeking an intervention order on me, I was working on extending the one I had on him. It would have been funny, if it hadn't been so frightening,

THE DATe for the hearing arrived, and I attended the police station as instructed before going into court. My co-worker Sue had kindly agreed to support me on the day. When we arrived, Marty was at the counter checking in, and afterwards he sat down in the front row and watched me. The clerk knew the situation and told me to step to my left and stand in front of the police room for safety. She said she would also tell Marty to leave and go upstairs. One of the Broadmeadows policemen approached me, pointed out the PSOs who patrol the waiting area and the area outside Legal Aid, and told me to run to them if I needed help. The tension was excruciating.

In the courtroom, I showed the magistrate and Marty's lawyer the footage I had taken, which Marty had greatly exaggerated. He claimed that I had followed him while I was filming, but the footage clearly shows that we had walked into him. At no point did we actually pursue him. Then Marty's lawyer took him outside to talk. When they came back, Marty said he had made a mistake and revised his accusations. Marty had also stated on the interim order that my ex-husband had told him I was manipulative and vindictive, and he was in fear for his life. I was appalled; Marty's lawyer was using hearsay to obtain an order.

I didn't have a lawyer; the list of lawyers the Law Institute had given me all had a conflict. Once again, I was representing myself. The hearing went on for ages as I was arguing against an order and determined to protest it to the end. The magistrate was fully aware I wanted nothing to do with Marty, yet he asked me to consider agreeing to an undertaking. I didn't want to do that—at that time I still didn't fully understand what an undertaking was. I argued repeatedly that I wanted the application for the intervention order dismissed, as I had done nothing wrong.

The day was dragging on and on. I felt that unless I agreed to an undertaking in lieu of the order I was never going to get out of there. The magistrate kept breaking off to hear other cases. It was becoming a long and stressful day and the magistrate would not let me leave until I agreed to the undertaking. At my first court appearance, I'd been lucky to have a sympathetic magistrate, but this time I was getting little support from the bench. And it wasn't the last time I would see this magistrate.

Eventually I agreed to the undertaking, as it seemed like that was the only way I could get out of there. But I wasn't happy. I now had an undertaking against my name for the next twelve months, without really knowing what that meant. To add insult to injury, as I was now considered the criminal I was asked to stay back in the courthouse so Marty could leave safely. Could this day have been any worse?

Sue and I were so late leaving that the courthouse was closed to the public and staff had to let us out. I sat in my car for some time, answering phone calls and messages. After I finally left and while I was stopped at a red light, I looked in my mirror and who should I see behind me but Marty. Obviously, he had waited for me. We had just been to court so he could legally force me to stay away from him, and here he was following me. I was beyond stressed. Why was he doing this? I called the police, who advised me not to take any more photos, as that is what had got me into trouble and into court. Marty was playing the victim, but I was the real victim and was somehow being blamed. I was exhausted and now had a legal document against my name, while Marty was doing whatever he wanted to me. I felt like my inter-vention order was worthless.

LATER THAT MONTH things finally seemed to turn in my favour. Police called and advised that they were charging Marty with a breach of my order based on his outburst at the police station when he 'suggested' I commit suicide. I was also glad to see Sergeant Williams at Craigieburn Central measuring 200 metres from the entrance of Big W.

Poor Rhiannon had hardly any hours on her learner permit because I wouldn't let her drive my car for fear it had been tampered with. But on 7 September, I calcu-lated that it had been two weeks since there had been any damage to my car. So when Rhiannon asked to drive to Shepparton on her birthday and get the hours up on her learner permit, I agreed. After dropping her off at her dad's in Mooroopna, I headed to Albury for a gig with the girls. It felt so good to relax and feel happiness again. And with the warmer weather, some of the remaining insulation foam melted off my car.

But this saga was far from over.

CHAPTER 4

POSTER GIRL

ON 28 SEPTEMBER, Marty attended court for breaking the intervention order on him the day he threatened my life at the police station. He was convicted, but he didn't go to jail. Instead, he paid a bond and agreed to take anger management classes. Marty had threatened my life, and this was all the punishment he got. I couldn't believe it.

I'd have been much happier if Marty had been locked up in jail where he couldn't touch me, but I had to get on with things. I began meeting with a victims' assistance group to get some help with lawyers and counsellors, and they couldn't believe I'd been doing this all on my own. I had also been referred to the women's help service run by Merri Health, and had a meeting with one of its staff at Sunbury Police Station.

Unsurprisingly, Marty's conviction failed to make him see sense, and he continued to interfere with my life. From time to time, I had mail go missing. Then an important parcel from eBay failed to arrive. Next were papers sent from Merri Health and my council rates notice. Then more parcels. It could have been just a coincidence, but it was easy to think I was being targeted because Rhiannon was receiving everything she ordered. I contacted Australia Post, but they were unable to help. Once again, I was banging my head against a brick wall.

I had also been trying to re-finance my mortgage and get a cheaper interest rate, but my credit report came back with a bad rating that had only been added two months ago. I had always paid my bills on time, until they started going missing. I was now getting very distressed, as Marty had had access to my house all those months ago before I changed the locks. What else was going to turn up? I called Merri Health in tears, but there was nothing they could do.

I continued to search for a lawyer, and continued to have no luck. Merri Health recommended someone, but she turned out to be Marty's lawyer. I called Merri Health for another recommendation, as the Women's Legal Service refused to help due to a 'conflict'. I wasn't always sure what the nature of these conflicts was, as these lawyers tended to hang up before I had a chance to find out more. The police had told me Marty's file was very extensive, so no wonder I was having trouble sourcing a lawyer.

It was now November 2015, and what I believe were Marty's attacks now began to target my family and friends. At 11.30 one night I was out for drinks with Cathie and some other friends when Mum called and said a rock had been thrown through her front window. I told her to call Triple Zero.

For my birthday in November, I decided to have the party of all parties to try and forget about everything that was happening. But I couldn't. While I was at the hairdresser getting myself ready for the party, Cathie rang to say Marty had left an offensive poster on the window of Elwood Food & Wine Bar. The same poster had also been left at the Winelarder. This time Marty had printed Cathie's phone number, offering my services for a particular sex act. The owner of Elwood Food & Wine Bar called the police to tell them he had footage of a man in a balaclava putting up the poster.

On 2 December I went to the police about the posters. We all knew Marty had put them up, because the formatting of the posters was just like the 'love' letters he had sent me when we were dating. I could also tell that the man in a balaclava in the CCTV footage was him because he has a distinctive walk as a result of back surgery. But from the police perspective none of this was proof that he'd put up the posters, so there was nothing they could do. Marty hadn't crossed the line far enough.

Meanwhile Marty was creating aliases and using them to leave bad comments on photos that friends had posted on my Facebook page. As soon as he created a new alias, I blocked it, but I couldn't keep up with them all. It was just a nightmare and I was feeling really frustrated with all of this. What was going to happen to make it stop? How much worse could this get?

IN JANUARY 2016, tragedy struck. My childhood friend Karen Chetcuti went missing. Five days later her body was found in bushland near Lake Buffalo. She had been brutally murdered. The horrific circumstances of her death resulted in a life sentence without possibility of parole for her murderer.

I was devastated by this news. How could a person inflict such torture on someone else? I connected with old school friends, and together we agreed to organise a fundraiser for Karen's family. We decided on a walk from our old high school in Blackburn South to the Burvale Hotel.

Supporters at the march for Karen Chetcuti included
my sister, Michelle, and friends Nancy & Lynette

I contacted my muso friends, and many of them agreed to perform at the hotel. Big W also offered items for a silent auction we planned to have at The Burvale. It's nice to know that in times of crisis, people band together. I did an interview with the *Herald Sun* with two of the other organisers, Wendy and Cheryl, and we also appeared on *A Current Affair* to promote the fundraiser.

The walk was scheduled for 21 February, which turned out to be a beautiful day. Many people took part, including some of Karen's friends from her childhood whom I had grown up with. Lots of media were there thanks to the report in the *Herald Sun*, which had published the route we were taking from the high school to the hotel. Even Derryn Hinch was there and helped carry a banner with my sister.

Marty must have also read the *Herald Sun* article. Someone—obviously Marty—had lined the route with offensive posters about me, which used the photo the *Herald Sun* had published with its article. The posters stated that I was a cheap whore, and that marching for Karen was an insult to 'genuine women that have morals'. Thankfully, the posters were found and pulled down before the march by Wendy's niece and her friends. If they hadn't been found and removed, it would have ruined the whole day.

THE ATTACKS ON me continued as 2016 rolled on, and Marty took no notice of the intervention order against him. I couldn't go to the supermarket without him being there. I asked the cashier at the express checkout to call security ASAP if he tried to attack me or cause trouble when I was there, but otherwise I just tried to ignore him and get the hell out of there.

One day I saw Marty out the front of my work hassling the owner of Showcase Jewellers. My intervention order didn't require Marty to stay 200 metres away from my workplace; apparently, his need to shop at Craigieburn Central was more important than my safety.

Around this time Mum started having trouble coping without Dad. After she had a serious fall, we decided to start looking at nursing homes for her. On 22 March, I left work at lunchtime to meet Mum and my sister to look at an aged care home. As I was driving along Fitz-simmons Lane in Eltham, who do I see alongside me? Marty. Was he following me?

There was an intersection in Templestowe where I needed to turn. Marty turned there, but I went straight ahead and took a photo of his car. Then I pulled over and rang Triple Zero and said he was following me. The police said they would send a car, but I thought that was useless as Marty would be long gone by the time the police arrived. It was impossible to stay even one step ahead of him.

Police from Heidelberg called me the next day to fol-low up my Triple Zero call. I went into Craigieburn Police Station to make a statement and give them the photo. They said it was probably a coincidence that Marty and I were in that part of Melbourne at the same time. Really? I told them I take the back streets to get to Blackburn South and visit my family, not the usual main roads. Why would Marty be driving down those streets? I also pointed out that it's a half-hour drive from Craigieburn to Blackburn South, and Marty had no reason to be there. Again, I was told it was a coincidence, and Marty was never questioned over this.

I asked the police again about having my car checked for a tracker, and again was told they were unable to do that because they didn't have the equipment. I'm not sure this is true, as years later the police did in fact search my car. Did they think I was simply being a nuisance?

A short time later Mum moved out of the family home and into the nursing home I had been on the way to see the day that Marty followed me. My cousins came over from Adelaide one weekend soon after that and we went to the football together. Afterwards we all went back to Mum's house, where my cousins were going to stay the night. We chatted for a while, then around midnight I set off for home. At 12:50 am, just as everyone was settling into their beds, a cricket ball was thrown through the loungeroom window. It just missed my cousin's young son, who was terrified and very upset. My cousins threw on some clothes and gave chase, but weren't quick enough to catch whoever did it. They did, however, see a guy limping down the street and getting into a white Commodore sedan.

My cousins called Triple Zero for help, then called me to explain what had happened. When they described the car, I knew it was Marty. I told my cousin I was going to get in my car and drive past Marty's house to see if his car was there. It wasn't. Had Marty followed me to Mum's house earlier?

The next day, Rhiannon and her boyfriend's mum, Sophie, had an altercation with Marty at Craigieburn Central. Sophie wound down her window to tell Marty to leave us alone, and later Sophie's house was egged. Sophie had cameras at her house, but sadly nothing showed up on them. If only I could get some hard evidence that Marty was behind these attacks.

On 25 April, Cathie received a hand delivered letter with the same style of type and a message similar to the previous offensive letters and posters that had been delivered or posted to the Winelarder, Elwood Food & Wine, and installed on the route for Karen Chetcuti's march. The only reason she checked her mailbox that day—which was a public holiday—was because her gate had been left open. Marty must have come inside her property and put the letter in her mailbox from the other side. It was awful to think he was creeping around and coming inside her gate like that.

I was severely distressed that Marty was now attacking people close to me. It was almost as if the intervention order had made things worse for my family and friends. Marty couldn't legally get close to me, but he could go after them. Making things worse was that the police were doing nothing. I once had a policewoman tell me the solution to my troubles would be to get a new phone number, new job and new house. What?! One day I rang the Domestic Violence Unit, and after a frustrating conversation I asked the policeman on the end of the line if he would help me when I was dead. He responded by hanging up.

I should point out that it wasn't always like this. When I went into Craigieburn Police Station to report the rock going through Mum's window and everything else that had happened that weekend, I spoke to a lovely policewoman who seemed to want to help me. Part of the problem was that too many police stations and police personnel had become involved. I felt like I needed someone in the police force to be my advocate, and that when I rang Triple Zero I needed a response in seconds, not minutes or hours.

Another problem was the lack of hard evidence. There was no way of proving that Marty was putting up the offensive flyers and posters, or that it was him in the CCTV footage we had. But perhaps what was most

Happier times with Celeste and Cathie

frustrating was the lack of understanding around stalking. Marty hadn't laid a finger on me, but you don't have to be physically attacked to be terrorised—this is what too many people fail to understand and where the law is not strong enough.

MAY 2016 WAS fairly quiet, but I continued to see Marty in places too close for comfort. One day I had to stop at the roundabout at the end of my street, just five houses away, and give way to Marty. I called the police, but as I didn't have any footage of the incident nothing could be done.

Later that month, I had an appointment to vary my intervention order against Marty and add addresses to it. Maybe that would help. The first hearing was adjourned because Marty hadn't been served with papers, and I was given a fresh court date of 23 May. I was requesting to have three addresses added: my mother's house in Blackburn South, Cathie's address in Brighton, and

Sophie's address in Craigieburn. I was pleased that the magistrate granted the changes to my order, but it was still due to expire on 4 July, after which I would have to apply for a new order.

My stress levels were through the roof and around this time my health took a turn for the worse. I ended up at the Austin Hospital having bloodwork, x-rays on my hands, and an MRI on my hips. I wasn't coping, and my stress point was my hips, which were excruciatingly painful. I was also booked in at the Mercy Hospital for a procedure after my pap smear had found some abnormal cells. Just one more thing for me to worry about. Stress seemed to be eating away at my body.

Cathie had also begun looking for a new place to live around this time; she'd had enough of everything happening at the house in Brighton. She had done many of her paintings at the old house, but she felt it was time to move on. Her relationship had also suffered, and she and her partner went their separate ways. Cathie found a lovely apartment a couple of suburbs away that offered good security. Her car, and mine when I visited, would be locked safely in an underground carpark. We had a final sleepover at her old place on 3 June, along with our friend Celeste, and spent the next day binge-watching Robert de Niro movies.

I desperately needed time away from my stalking nightmare; a break from constantly looking over my shoulder wondering if I was going to be attacked or worrying about my car. I'd been dating a man called Henry for a while, and took some leave from work so we could go to Hamilton Island for a week. Henry and I had a wonderful, relaxing time, staying in a beautiful bungalow, enjoying the sunshine and peaceful life on the island. I really didn't want to come home. But sadly, I had to.

It was also time for me to leave my job. With the stress I was under causing so many health issues, I decided it was best to find a more private and secure workplace where I wouldn't be under the constant threat of Marty turning up and causing trouble. I didn't want to leave the job I adored; I had been at Big W for eight years, I loved the people I worked with, and they loved me. They had my back, and to this day, they still do. But on 30 June, 2016, I went to Big W for the last time. It was a very emotional day for us all, but I had to consider my health.

Through contacts, I was lucky to get another job quite quickly—this time in fleet management. The company offered so much security: you needed a pass to get in and out of the workplace, so only staff were able to access the office. It would mean a long commute into the city and back every day, with long hours and a pay cut. The pay cut was a challenge for me as a single mother, especially since I was spending so much money on security at my house and repairs for my car. But at least I wouldn't be looking around for Marty to appear at any moment. I felt like I could breathe again while I was at work. I could relax.

I WAS BACK in court on 4 July to apply for another intervention order on Marty. Cathie came over to stay at my house so she could come to court with me. I didn't want Henry coming with me, as I had shielded him from all of this and I needed to keep him safe, although I'm sure Marty already knew about him.

While Cathie was staying at my place, we went out to grab some food. Cathie wanted to know where Marty lived and asked me to drive past his house. I thought this was a terrible idea—it WAS a terrible idea. But dear Cathie could be incredibly persuasive. I kept saying no, but she kept insisting that she wanted to see Marty's house. We ended up getting into a heated argument over it, and eventually I agreed to show her the house just so we could have some peace. Reluctantly, I drove quickly past Marty's house. Cathie complained it was too fast, so I reluctantly drove past one more time. Then Cathie wanted to go past yet again, and again I refused. We were pulled over in the next street, arguing, when I noticed headlights coming down the street. You guessed it—it was Marty. We sat frozen, not speaking, in my car. He slowed down as he went past, then we started screaming, 'Oh my God, oh my God!' Marty had turned left, but only into the side street. He turned around and came back to see if we were still there, and yes, we were. I then did a U-turn, and we got the hell out of there, both of us freaking out and screaming at each other. If you ever have a stalker, do NOT do anything like this.

The next day I was in court, and yet again I had to represent myself, as I still hadn't been able to find a lawyer who didn't have a conflict. Cathie and I went into the courtroom, and I was very pleased to see that sitting behind the bench was the same magistrate who had granted my original order. I also noticed that Marty wasn't there.

The magistrate asked the clerk where Marty was, and whether he had been served. They determined that Marty had been served and had failed to appear, but fortunately he didn't need to be there. Magistrate Bentley asked me what evidence I had and why I wanted a continuation of the order. I gave him five flyers that suggested I should be raped or worse. Then Magistrate Bentley started talking to himself. He was saying, 'I remember this case, I remember this case.' Then, 'Ten years, ten years.' He kept saying, 'Ten years.' I didn't understand what was happening, and looked at the clerk for guidance, but he had no clue what was going on. Eventually I had to ask, 'Is that a ten-year order, Your Honour?' And Magistrate Bentley said, 'Yes.'

I couldn't believe my ears, and I don't think the clerk could either. The order covered my house, Cathie's house, Sophie's house, my parent's house, Rhiannon's school and workplace, my former workplace (Big W) to the front door, and five metres in a public place until 2026. I was stunned. Magistrate Bentley instructed me to wait outside, and the clerk would be out with the paperwork. I thanked him, walked out of the courtroom, and broke down in tears.

CHAPTER 5

TERROR AND TRAGEDY

ON 11 JULY 2016, I started my new job. The office was in the city, so I had to catch a train. Normally I would use Craigieburn station, but I didn't want Marty to know where I was or to attack my car while I was at work, so I drove down the Hume Highway to Donnybook station and caught a V-Line train. It seemed ridiculous that I couldn't use my local train station and catch a suburban train now that I had a ten-year order against Marty, but I had learnt that an IVO was no guarantee that he would leave me alone.

And he didn't.

Rhiannon and I were out shopping one day when Marty drove past us really slowly. We kept walking and tried to ignore him, but then I wondered about Rhiannon's car so we doubled back to see if he had stopped there. We were relieved to see he was nowhere near the car, but the paranoia we were experiencing was taking its toll.

Then more flyers were left at the Winelarder and Elwood Food & Wine. This time they targeted me and

Cathie, calling us Dumb and Dumber and Tweedle Dee and Tweedle Dum.

Rhiannon was in the middle of VCE exams around this time. One evening I got a frantic phone call from her to say Marty was in the library where she had gone to study. He was at the computer doing God knows what— printing offensive flyers about me, I expect. I went to the library and found that Rhiannon was really stressed, saying that Marty wouldn't leave. Rhiannon was on my order, so Marty should have left when she walked in. He was flagrantly ignoring the IVO conditions by remaining in the library. Rhiannon had an exam in the morning, and had thought she would be safe at the library because we knew Marty only went there during the day. I nervously approached Marty and asked him to leave. He wouldn't. I called Triple Zero, but the police didn't come. Instead they asked me to give Marty my phone. I refused, as I didn't want him putting a tracker on my new phone. Instead I put the policeman on speaker, and he instructed Marty to call him. The incident ended with Marty walking around the library, screaming down his phone at the policeman. Rhiannon and I left with the security guard walking us to my car. Poor Rhiannon never got to do what she wanted to, and was so traumatised by the whole event she didn't go to her exam the next day.

I also broke up with Henry, the man I had been seeing, around this time. He said, 'It's not you, it's me,' but I'm not so sure. I wasn't the person I used to be.

ONE WEEK INTO 2017, Marty hit the venues again with more flyers. I went to Craigieburn Police Station on Sunday 15 January to hand them in, and who should walk in behind me but Marty. It was very unnerving because the counter was unattended. We were waiting around for some time, and Marty was looking at what I had in my hand and staring at me intensely. It was quite unnerving. I told Marty he had serious mental issues and he was now involving other people. Then I got my phone out to call the station as no one was coming out and I was standing there unprotected. I was also supposed to go to Cathie's, but texted her to say I had to go home.

When a policeman finally appeared, Marty ran to the counter, screaming, 'That woman has serious mental problems.' I told the policeman that I had a ten-year order on this clown. He looked at me, then at Marty, then offered me a safe room. I declined, saying I would come back after Marty had gone. I had recently bought a new car—it was one positive action I could take to protect myself—and I didn't want Marty knowing what I was driving. This tactic proved fruitless, however. When I went back to the station to make a statement, the police checked their cameras and found that Marty had been two cars behind me when I first pulled into the carpark. So, he already knew I had a new car. The officer asked me if I had a dash cam, and suggested I move it to the rear window so I could record who was following me.

Following this incident, Marty was charged with breaking the intervention order and had to appear in court on 31 March. The hearing was later adjourned to May,

Throughout this time, my bestie, Cathie, continued to prop me up. She'd send little messages saying, *'Sending you big kisses and hugs…Hopefully soon Marty will be in jail… Focus on the good.'* I don't know what I would have done without her, and the first thing I did when I got home after Marty broke the order at Craigieburn Police Station was call Cathie. But she didn't answer. I tried her again, but still no answer. I gave up and went to bed, exhausted, and tried to sleep after a very hectic, stressful day.

THE FOLLOWING DAY, Monday 16 January, I received a message from Christine at the Winelarder while I was at work. She told me she had heard that Cathie had committed suicide. I was gobsmacked. I couldn't believe my eyes. Suddenly my emotions were all over the shop. My heart began to race and I had a sinking feeling in my stomach. It was 10 am, and although I hadn't spoken to Cathie over the weekend, I thought it must be a mistake and tried to ring her. No answer. I started to panic. I was absolutely terrified that it might be true.

I called our friends Maurice and Celeste. I told Maurice no one could get hold of Cathie, and he said to call her local police station. I called Bayside Police Station and asked for Adam Williamson, who had attended Cathie's home many times. He said there were no suicide reports for her address, and did I want them to do a welfare check? I said yes. Then I spoke to my manager, who told me to just go, as my mind obviously wasn't on work. I called Steve, a friend who had been dating Cathie, and asked him to head to Cathie's as well. He told me that he and Cathie were supposed to catch up on Saturday night, but things had got away from him at work and he never made it.

I was now even more frantic, as no one had seen or heard from Cathie all weekend. I left work and rang Steve again, who was already at Cathie's but said there was no answer when he knocked. He told me to get in a taxi and come over. I had a key and would be able to let us in. In the taxi, I got a call from Maurice. He had spoken to another mutual friend, who had more information. 'She's gone, she's gone, Di. Don't go in her house. She's gone.'

When I got to Cathie's I found Steve sitting on the front stairs. We decided not to go inside, and sat there wondering what to do. I felt numb. We went to the Winelarder,

The last, home-made, birthday card Cathie gave me

but it was closed. I didn't want to be alone, so I called
Maurice and asked if I could come round. Later a bunch
of us met up at Sons of Mary in Brighton to talk and talk,
and cry, and at times sit in silence. I took several days off

work, feeling numb and crying a lot. Every now and then I'd call Cathie's phone to hear her voice.

CATHIE'S SONS HAD found her body on 15 January, the day I was in the police station dealing with Marty. Why had he stared at me so intently? Did he know? Was he wondering how I would react to the death of my best friend? If he did know, how did he know? To this day, I don't believe Cathie committed suicide, and I'm not the only one of her friends who thinks this. She had been through a lot worse than what was going on at that time. We always got together in hard times and supported each other when we were feeling down. Why hadn't Cathie reached out this time? This is why I don't think she took her own life. I will go to my grave believing this, but I can't prove anything; I have to accept the coroner's findings.

Cathie was my best friend, and I felt lost without her. There was so much going on in my life, but I no longer had someone to bounce off and keep me sane. To this day, I miss our daily calls and messages. I have friends— good friends—but she was the Patsy to my Edina; she was my Ab Fab. She got me. We teased each other; we laughed and cried and partied together; and we looked after each other. We had each other's backs. But now she was gone.

CATHIE WAS GONE; my stalker wasn't. The Winelarder continued to receive offensive posters and letters. On 28 January, I went over to the Winelarder and spoke to Christine about the latest 'deliveries'. She didn't know how to tell me about these new posters, and had had them for a while. This was unusual; Christine usually messaged me the day the posters were left. I soon found out why—the posters were all about Cathie's death.

They said things like 'RIP Cathie' and 'the wrong woman passed away'. The letters accused me of having blood on my hands and killing Cathie. I went around to Elwood Food & Wine Bar, and found out they had received the same letters. There was CCTV footage of 'the offender' putting up the letters at 1.55am on 21 January, 2017. I took all the posters and letters to Craigieburn Police Station and spent hours making a three-page statement.

On 22 April, I'd been up to Shepparton for the day and arrived home around 9 pm. It had been a long day, Rhiannon was at her boyfriend's, and by 10 pm I was in bed with the TV on. I was dozing off when a loud bang sounded. I thought, what was that? Was it a tree branch falling on the roof? Then I realised I don't have trees large enough for that to be a possibility. I got up, rang Triple Zero and went into the office to look at the feed from my CCTV cameras. I rewound the footage as I was talking to the operator on the phone, and the cameras showed a masked man walking across the street and coming towards my house. He ducked behind my arbour, then peeked around it. His eyes were glowing. I was terrified and screamed at the operator to send someone. She told me to calm down. I said to her, 'You're not seeing what I'm seeing. Please send the police.' They never came.

The next day I went into Craigieburn Police Station and made another statement. I also shared the footage from my cameras on several Craigieburn Facebook pages, asking for residents in my area to keep a lookout for a man wearing a balaclava. I also asked if anyone saw the man at around 10.30—11 pm on the previous night. I put the same footage up on my personal Facebook page, and Rhiannon put it up on hers as well. If the police couldn't help me, I would have to help myself.

I arranged to have roller shutters installed on my windows, and thankfully this was done within days. I bought some security lights, and the guy installing the shutters put them up for me as well. Such a nice thing for him to do. I told him my story, and he was horrified. I was grateful that the company he worked for understood my anxiety and fear and cleared their schedule to install the shutters.

It wasn't long before I heard another loud bang on my roof late at night. I'd been out with my friends Maurice and Celeste, who called me later to make sure I'd got home safely. I was on the phone with Celeste, who also heard the bang on the other end of the line. I hung up and called the police. Once again, they didn't show.

Shortly after this I had an appointment with my hairdresser, Jacki, who had been doing my hair since 2014. I started talking about going to court and all the dramas that had been happening. Jacki was in shock, as she didn't know about me being stalked. But I was even more shocked to learn that Marty had been going to the same salon since late 2016. When he first went there, one of the other girls did his hair, but then he started asking for Jacki. Worse, Marty had been complaining to her about a woman who was making false allegations about him and taking him to court all the time. He didn't use my name, but it was obviously me. Poor Jacki was now nervous about Marty coming in, and I would have to find another hairdresser. This might sound like a small thing, but Marty was forcing me to change my habits and behaviour in countless ways. It was like death by a thousand cuts.

On 8 May I was in court again for Marty's breach of the intervention order in January, when he followed me into Craigieburn Police Station and told the police officer at the counter that I had 'serious mental issues'. He

Rhiannon, me, Celeste and Maurice in Calabasas,
California. The only time I could relax was
when there was an ocean between me and Marty

asked for and was granted another adjournment, with a new court date of 8 June. Marty did this constantly—adjourning hearings for petty reasons and delaying the court process. It would take six or seven months for this particular matter to be resolved, with the matter being struck out. Apparently IVOs do not apply to police stations, just as they don't apply to courts of law, and when Marty came into the station it was not technically a breach. When the hearing was adjourned to June I thought, great, I would be in LA and would miss this one.

A few weeks earlier my friends Celeste and Maurice had invited Rhiannon and I to visit them in LA. I was over everything—tired, not sleeping, waking at every little sound. I needed a break, and LA seemed like a brilliant idea. So in early June 2017, Rhiannon and I left for LA. I had a blissful time there and wasn't aware of what was going on back in Melbourne. Little did I know that every time I changed my cover photo or profile pic on Facebook, Marty used it to create another flyer defaming me.

Back in Melbourne, it was just hours before Marty struck again. I'd gone to pick up my puppy from my family, and noticed in my rear-view mirror that there was a white car driving up quickly behind us. I said to Rhiannon that if the car turns when we do, then it's probably Marty. I turned into my street and stopped at the roundabout. Sure enough, the car did the same. And there he was behind the wheel, where we could all see him. How did he know I was there? I stopped long enough to get some footage of Marty in his car, and was glad I'd had Rhiannon and her boyfriend in the car as witnesses. I went home and called the police.

After we got home from LA it was around Cathie's birthday. I organised a night at the Winelarder with friends a few days later to mark the occasion, and we ate and drank, enjoyed good music and told our Cathie stories. It was something we all needed to do; we needed to celebrate her life. I especially needed to do that, otherwise I would have been home alone, depressed and drinking and worrying about my stalker—who wasn't letting up.

The next batch of flyers Marty posted featured a photo I had posted on Facebook of me standing in front of Eddie Van Halen's guitar at Hard Rock Hollywood. The caption called me a 'second rate hooker'.

BY THIS TIME, I had become more than a little disillusioned with the system. The courts were a nightmare, the law seemed to protect Marty more than it did me, and the police, although they often tried to help, just as often let me down. It was time to look outside the system for help.

I had joined a Facebook group called Protect Victoria in June 2017, which was organising a forum for the following month to talk to the two main political parties about the state of crime in Melbourne. Sadly, no one from the Labor party attended and only Liberal politicians were there. The *Today Show* was going to be there filming as well. After work, I drove to Carnegie for the forum.

I didn't put my hand up during the filming, as I was trying to stay out of sight; I didn't want Marty seeing me on the *Today Show* when it aired. After the forum ended, I approached Matthew Guy, then leader of the Opposition, and Ed O'Donohue, who at the time was the Shadow Police Minister, and told them my story. I had taken with me some printed excerpts from my 2015 diary to hand out, and gave one each to Matthew Guy, Ed O'Donohue, John Pesutto and a few others in the Liberal Party.

Within days, I had a phone call from Glenn Corey, who worked for Ed and whom I had also met at the forum. That day proved to be pivotal in my story. Ed and Glenn were to become a catalyst for change. Ed contacted Police Minister Lisa Neville and told her my story. She in turn contacted Broadmeadows Police Station to find out why I wasn't getting any help, and why these attacks were still happening. I was assigned a policewoman, and the sergeant also contacted me. We had a meeting at Broadmeadows Police Station on a Saturday, which the sergeant came in for especially. I thought, here we go; I finally have help.

But there was still a long way to go.

CHAPTER 6

ROUND AND ROUND THE COURTS WE GO

JUST WHEN I thought I might finally get some real help and some traction on making all the madness stop, Marty had me served with papers to appear in court. The hearing was scheduled for 4 October 2017. He was applying for an intervention order against me—for the second time. Yes, the man who refused to stay away from me and had been stalking and terrorising me, my family and my friends for three years, was claiming that *I* was a threat to *his* safety.

He claimed that I had put up a Facebook post using his picture and inciting violence against him. I guessed this was in retaliation for me posting footage on Facebook of the man in a balaclava out the front of my house. I had put this footage on several different Facebook Craigieburn pages, and also Protect Victoria's page. It was ludicrous—how could I incite violence against a man who could not be identified by the picture I posted? I was sure it was Marty—everybody was—but I never named him in the posts. The real absurdity in all of this, obviously, was that by claiming I was inciting violence against him Marty had essentially identified himself!

This time I was desperate to find a lawyer to represent me. I made phone call after phone call, and even tried the Women's Legal Service again. I had forgotten they had a conflict, and was beside myself. He was a man, it was a *women's* service—how could they possibly have a conflict? They declined to elaborate on the reasons.

I did have great support through all of this from my co-workers, both at Big W and at my new job. I had obtained another list of lawyers who might be able to help me from my local Member of Parliament (MP), and one day my manager told me to go into a meeting room, start making phone calls, and not come out until I had found a lawyer. So I did. I got all the way down to the Ys before I found someone who could represent me.

On the day of the hearing I arrived at court with Luke, my newly acquired lawyer, not knowing what this Facebook post was all about as Marty's lawyer hadn't given us a copy. Luke had to go to the clerk at the front desk to get a copy of the 'evidence' that had been submitted. When I saw it, I knew immediately that it was a fake. Marty had cut and pasted photos of himself onto a printout of my Facebook post and claimed it was real. In fact, the post didn't exist.

Luke explained this to the magistrate who, I was dismayed to see, was the same one who had pressured me into signing an undertaking the first time Marty applied for an IVO against me. Marty's lawyer kept saying that once a Facebook post is on the world wide web, it's there forever. But it was a fake post; it had never been on the web. Luke kept trying to explain this, but the magistrate said that fact was neither here nor there. As far as he was concerned, the paperwork in front of him amounted to me inciting violence against Marty, and whether it was on Facebook or not was irrelevant.

How could the magistrate not understand that Marty had created the 'paperwork', not me? Did he not realise he was being lied to? Marty was the one with an intervention order on him, not to mention a conviction for breaking it and, as I later discovered, a long history of stalking and harassing women with convictions going back to the 1980s. My record was clean, yet the magistrate believed Marty. It was unfair and outrageous.

The magistrate asked Luke to take me outside to make me 'see sense' and take the order. I was furious. Luke went to the counter to find out the earliest date I could be back in court to fight the application. I would have to wait until February 2018 to contest the order, and then have to go to court again in June for another hearing. It would be nine months before I could get this monkey off my back. I would also need a barrister for these hearings, meaning Luke would be unable to represent me. Marty already had an interim order on me that would be in place until I could get a court date, so essentially I would go through all that stress, time and expense to contest the order only to reduce it by a few months. And that was assuming that I could successfully contest it. It was possible that I would lose my case and the magistrate would give me the order for another twelve months, starting from the final court date. Maybe I should cut my losses and save some money.

Giving Marty what he wanted made me sick to my stomach, but fighting it seemed both pointless and expensive. We went back in, and Luke advised the magistrate that I would take the order without admission.

The magistrate's response was to look at me, smirk—yes, smirk—and say that had I appealed it, he would have given me an order regardless. I was speechless.

Marty had got what he wanted, but now he wanted more. He started arguing with the magistrate for a ten-year order on me. Thankfully, the magistrate refused, saying he didn't hand out orders that long. I believe that was Marty's plan all along—because I had a ten-year order on him, he wanted one on me and was willing to do anything to get it. Tit for tat.

To this day, I am reeling that the magistrate didn't believe me that the Facebook post wasn't real, that he didn't look into it further. I have all the original posts, but didn't have them on the day as I didn't know I would need them. I was blindsided, and Marty won again. I would now have an intervention order on me until September 2018.

It's because of this that I shut down my Facebook page, which meant I wouldn't have reminders popping up of my life with Cathie, or memories of my children from their childhood. It was heartbreaking. But by having an active Facebook page I was unwittingly feeding Marty information, and he was using it for his own gain. He was manipulating my life to make out I was attacking him. This had to stop. So I shut my life down.

BEFORE I KNEW IT, it was 2018. I hoped that this sad story would soon end, but on 2 January the Winelarder and Elwood Food & Wine both received more offensive flyers about me. Chris from the Winelarder contacted me about them while I was on holiday in Queensland. The only time I could truly relax during this period was when I was in another state or another country. I was trying to have a peaceful time on a cruise, but my shitty life still haunted me. I tried to focus on the cruise, and not let Marty get inside my head.

At the end of January I was due in court. This was for the breach back in June, when Marty had followed me after arriving back from LA. I decided not to go, but the hearing was adjourned until 28 February. Apparently Marty had an excuse, but I was unable to find out what it was. Eight months later, and we were still on the court merry-go-round.

Meanwhile, Marty's attacks had continued. Through-out the second half of 2017 more flyers had gone up, I heard more bangs on my roof in the middle of the night, and Marty was seen at Rhiannon's workplace. All these happenings meant more visits to the police so they could take more statements. It was exhausting. I also started receiving hang-up phone calls on my landline, which worried me as I had a silent number. I also found out that Marty had been asking my old hairdresser where I was going now to get my hair done. These sound like harmless little facts, but when you have a stalker you can never be sure that a strange occurrence is just a strange occurrence and not something more sinister.

The stress was continuing to affect me physically. I had one tooth break, then another. My dentist was in awe of my broken tooth, as he had only seen such a case in textbooks, and took a lot of photos. The tooth was near the front and I didn't want a gap there—even if I didn't smile much anymore—so the dentist fixed it as best he could. It wasn't perfect, but it was better than the alter-native, which was losing the tooth altogether.

MARTY HAD BEEN stalking me for three years, and I was becoming increasingly disillusioned with the police and the court system, especially after the farcical hearing in which Marty was granted his second intervention order against me. I realised that to get the help I needed, I'd have to think outside the box and not always rely on police. I began to look at other avenues for protection.

One thing I could do to give me some peace of mind was check my house for bugs and hidden cameras. I got in touch with a bug detection agency who said they would come over and do a sweep of my house. Half of me wanted them to find something, which would mean I wasn't crazy to be worrying about all this. The other half wanted them to find nothing, so I wasn't freaking out over what Marty might be doing with any photos or footage he had or conversations he had recorded. I was feeling sick to my stomach, but the peace of mind it would bring would be wonderful.

On the day of the inspection, Alan from Bug Detector arrived around 10am. I told him why I needed my home checked and what my fears were. My main concern was that Marty was watching Rhiannon in the shower. I wasn't concerned about myself, as I'm old and not in the best shape, but I was worried what he might do if he had filmed Rhiannon. Alan was at my home for three and a half hours. He was extremely thorough and also checked my car. Thankfully, he found nothing. My peace of mind cost me $1,100 but was well worth it. I actually had a decent night's sleep. Heaven.

THE NEXT STOP on the merry-go-round of court appearances was the adjourned hearing for Marty's breach of the intervention order back in June 2017, when he followed me after I returned from LA. The date was set for 28 February.

For some reason, I had a bad feeling about what might transpire that day. Rhiannon was working at the Big W store in Broadmeadows Central and I was worried about her safety. I rang Ash from security at the shopping centre and asked her to be especially vigilant that day and be on the look out for Marty. I said it was just a feeling and that I was probably over-reacting, but I would feel better if I knew Ash was in my corner. Ash had been amazing throughout the whole saga, and had a copy of my intervention order and photos of Marty. With Ash keeping watch I felt my girl would be in safe hands.

On advice from the prosecutor, I didn't attend the hearing on 28 February, but was in contact with a reporter called Jess who would be in court that day.

In court, Marty represented himself. He told the magistrate that he wasn't driving his car; it was a good friend of his who had come to his house to install a new oven. The friend discovered he needed parts to finish the job, so borrowed Marty's car to go to the nearest Bunnings. This information turned up late in the proceedings, and the magistrate said they would adjourn the hearing again until 22 March so they could have the correct person testify that they were driving.

Jess rang me to tell me what had happened. I was horrified. If Marty's 'friend' was going to Bunnings, he was driving in the wrong direction. Instead of turning left to follow me, he should have turned right. Did the magistrate not know that I had footage and witnesses to confirm who was driving? I received this news while I was still at work and was so upset that my manager offered to drive me home.

When I got back home, I discovered that the bad feeling I'd had that morning was justified. Ash called me to advise that Marty had headed straight over to Rhiannon's workplace after the court hearing. She asked me to call the police and advise them that Marty had attended the Big W where Rhiannon worked and had asked two staff members, one of them a manager, for her. He had spent nine minutes in the store looking for my daughter. This was a brazen breach of the intervention order. I was horrified, and terrified for the safety of my child.

I rang the police that were assigned to me, and none of them were there. In fact, they had been transferred. The poor officer who answered the phone and told me this copped an earful from me, but I was beside myself.

I then contacted Ed O'Donohue's office and spoke to Glenn Corey. He asked me to email details of everything that had happened and said he'd get Ed to pass it on to Lisa Neville and the Police Commissioner. I can tell you I was not calm; I dropped the 'F' bomb many, many times. Thankfully, Ed kept his word and passed on all the relevant information to Lisa Neville.

The next day, Rhiannon had three phone calls at work. The girl on the switchboard didn't know if Rhiannon was at work and asked the caller to leave a message, which they didn't. The switchboard person thought it sounded like 'an old guy'.

On Saturday 3 March, I took Rhiannon to Broadmeadows Police Station to make a statement about these events. Big W also gave her a copy of their CCTV footage, and Ash had already supplied police with the footage of Marty from the centre. At the police station I saw the footage for the first time. It was so creepy, watching Marty looking around and asking for Rhiannon with his court papers still in his hand. What was he doing there? Why was he wanting Rhiannon? What did he have planned for my daughter?

The next development in the saga of Marty's breach of the IVO in June 2017 came when my case worker at Broadmeadows rang to advise that Marty had changed his plea to guilty, and he would be convicted and face a large fine. I asked what happened to the statutory declaration that Marty's friend who had allegedly been driving his car was supposed to sign. I was told the friend had refused. Marty must have perjured himself, and yet he was never held accountable for this or for presenting false documents and wasting the court's and everyone else's time.

The next day, I called the police and found that Marty was fined $800, which they called quite extensive— apparently breach fines were usually only $100-$200. Maybe so, but it seemed a pittance compared to the torment I had suffered for the nine months since the charge had first been laid. It felt like a slap in the face. On 6 March, I decided to take a few days of stress leave.

On 13 March, as a result of contacting Ed O'Donohue, Lisa Neville organised a meeting for me with Sergeant Nick De Ridder and Detective Senior Constable Rebecca Norris from Broadmeadows Family Violence Unit. I went to the meeting hoping I wouldn't be let down again, hoping that this time, something concrete would come out of it. One of the first things Detective Norris, whom I would soon start calling Beck, did for me was put me in touch with Berry St, a family services organisation that helps people experiencing poverty, violence and abuse. Berry St were able to help me with an application I was making to Victims of Crime. They also stepped in when I was having trouble with cameras I'd installed in my house. And more help was on its way. Having Nick, and especially Beck, in my corner would prove to be the first step in turning the tide against Marty.

The next step in the legal merry-go-round was dealing with Marty's breach when he went looking for Rhiannon at Big W, on 28 February. Weeks went by as we waited for police to arrest him. Finally, on 17 April, Sergeant Nick De Ridder rang to advise that Marty had been arrested and charged and would appear before the courts for this matter on 27 April. Meanwhile he was out on bail but remanded to his home.

Police were expecting him to disobey his bail conditions, so I messaged all my neighbours to be on high alert in case Marty appeared in our street, and if they saw him, not to approach him but to call Triple Zero. I rang my old hairdresser as well, who had been cutting Marty's hair, and told her she should call the police if he came in. Finally I contacted Ash at Broadmeadows Central security and asked her to look out for Marty. I had everyone on high alert. Fear had set in. I was waiting to be attacked.

Thank goodness I had a loyal and supportive family. My sister and her family came over to help me put up a shed and tidy up my garden. I needed a break and to have people around me. It sounds like such a tiny, unimportant thing, but I needed these little interludes to keep me sane.

I also needed a change. I saw my new hairdresser and she changed me back to the blonde I had been eleven years before. My hair had turned white with all the stress, which made being blonde again an easy choice! I felt like a new person, and ready for the next chapter in the saga that my life had become.

ON 25 MAY, my friend Tess came to stay with me as I had court the next day. This hearing was for Marty's breach on 28 February against Rhiannon. I was starting to think I should rent a room at Broadmeadows Magistrates Court with the number of times I'd been there. Tess and I went into court, only to be told proceedings were adjourned. Apparently, Marty's lawyer had a previous engagement and was unable to attend. No one had told me.

Meanwhile the offensive posters and flyers continued to appear. A week after the adjourned court hearing, Beck emailed and asked when I was last at Elwood Food & Wine Bar and where I had sat. She had received word from Peter at the bar about more flyers. She would get him to look at his cameras and Bayside police would pick up the flyers. It seemed that now I had Beck assigned to my case, I didn't have to do all of the exhausting legwork: picking up flyers, making statements, asking for CCTV footage. Beck was very hands on and I felt the tide was turning.

On 6 June, Marty breached his bail conditions by going back to Big W at Broadmeadows. Ash from security caught him in front of the store, filming on his phone. I was so glad to have her in my corner! When Ash confronted Marty, he ran, claiming she had the wrong person. He started to duck and weave as he ran out of the centre, presumably to avoid being caught on the cameras— which was impossible. Ash went straight into Big W to see if Rhiannon was there; she was, and she had just gone upstairs for her tea break. As soon as Ash walked in, Rhiannon exclaimed, 'What now?!' Marty's harassment had become part of our lives—in a bad way. What would it take to make this stop?

One good thing about Marty breaching his bail conditions was that it was another black mark against him, and another step on the road to hopefully putting him behind bars. But waiting for the police to arrest him again was nerve wracking. Finally, after being on the loose for a week and having us all jumping at our own shadows, Marty was arrested for breaching bail. He was charged with stalking Rhiannon, breaching his intervention order and an extra charge of breaching his bail conditions—three charges in total. He was put in remand and due to appear in court on 15 June.

We couldn't wait for the hearing. It seemed that a jail sentence was the only thing that could stop Marty from attacking me and my friends and family. The original court document requested seven months in jail, and it looked like Marty was finally going to be locked up.

Sadly, the hearing proved to be something of an anticlimax. The magistrate handed down a three-month sentence—disappointing to say the least. Marty also appealed the sentence, and was released on appeals bail. To me, this made no sense—why would you grant bail to someone who had already breached the original bail conditions? How many chances would he get? We now had to wait until 23 August for the appeals hearing. This was such a joke.

AS THE DATE of the appeals hearing approached, Andrew Bosco (who was covering for Beck Norris while she was on leave) contacted me in regard to Rhiannon's victim impact statement. Rhiannon said she didn't want to read it aloud in court, and wanted just the judge to read it privately. I wanted Marty to wonder what she wrote, to watch him squirm. On 23 August, the day of the hearing in the County Court, we were asked again if Rhiannon wanted to read out her statement, and we reiterated our preference and the reasons for it. I was disappointed to learn that Marty had received a copy of Rhiannon's statement, and that he was in a room nearby reading it as we spoke. I was very upset that he was able to learn of my child's innermost feelings. Apparently, Marty had a right to know what was being said against him and to defend himself. I'm sorry, but where were our rights as victims? I felt like we had none.

Inside the courtroom, the presiding judge reduced Marty's sentence to one month in jail, followed by an eighteen-month good behaviour bond. Should he breach any of the conditions, it would be an automatic six months in jail. I had experienced untold stress and heart-ache to get Marty put away for just one month. It seemed ridiculous...

I was losing faith in the justice system. Marty had received a good behaviour bond for threats against my life, and now he received a one-month sentence and another good behaviour bond for going after a child. And in fact he never went to jail, but spent the entire month in the remand centre.

NEEDLESS TO SAY, our one month of freedom from worry over Marty passed in the blink of an eye. He was released from prison on 18 September. It was a nice present for Rhiannon, whose birthday is around that time.

Shortly after Marty was released I was on my way to work and saw him walking down the middle of the street. I had to stop, or I would have hit him. The street was close to my house, not his, and it was before seven in the morning. I rang Rhiannon to warn her that Marty was out and about, and to call Triple Zero should she feel endangered. I also gave her a description of what Marty was wearing: a pale blue hoody with a pattern on it.

At this time there were six days left on Marty's inter-vention order against me. I had been stressing over this, as I was worried that he would try to extend it. I'd booked a much-needed holiday in Bali for what I was calling my 'freedom' day, and checked with Beck to make sure I'd be able to go as I was worried about any court hearings. Poor Beck, I was emailing her constantly about my concerns. I told her about Marty's appearance, and also asked her if I should look at getting an IVO against Marty for Amity. Amity had moved back to Melbourne from Queensland, and when the house she was renting was sold she had moved in with Rhiannon and me. There was so much to worry about, I was making myself physically ill.

I was relieved when 3 October arrived and I hadn't received any court documents, meaning the order against me had expired and Marty had not sought to renew it. That meant Rhiannon and I were off to Bali for a few days. A friend had organised for us to have breakfast in the Qantas Business Lounge before our flight. While we were there, a page went out over the intercom. It was a page for a Marty Norman, who was wanted at reception for a phone call. Rhiannon bolted out of the ladies', yelling "Muuuummmm did you hear that!!!" Of course I had heard it; I felt ill. We went to reception to see if Marty was there. Thank God he wasn't. Obviously he had rung the Qantas lounge and asked for the page, which meant he somehow knew we were there. What a way to start our holiday...

CHAPTER 7

CONVICTION

IN NOVEMBER 2018 I was back from Bali, and wondering how all of this was going to end. Beck Norris was still trying to obtain evidence to charge Marty with more offences—the kind of offences that would put him in jail and keep him there for more than a measly month—and meanwhile I kept being attacked.

One night after work, the neighbour who lived behind me, Selina, came over to tell me she'd seen a strange man in a blue hoody walking our fence line. Selina had rung Triple Zero, but the police never showed up. A week later, I saw Marty walking around near our street again. On 11 November, Amity was in the backyard at around 9 pm when a drone suddenly appeared and started hovering around. Next, Rhiannon's car was egged. Early in the new year, I was spending a weekend in Rosebud with my sister, and as I was driving down the main road who should fly up my arse but Marty. Another time a former work colleague messaged me to say that Marty was at Big W in Craigieburn Central, looking for someone and running around like a madman. They were all too scared to intervene, and hoped that he would leave the store quickly.

Fortunately, behind the scenes, I was finally getting real help from the police.

When Beck Norris was put in charge of my case, she investigated Marty's past. She found that he had been stalking women for decades. At least five other women had at one time had IVOs against Marty. But as each woman decided—for whatever reason—not to pursue legal action against him, he was free to move on to another victim. I hoped that at least one of these women would come out of the woodwork and join forces with me to fight against Marty, but sadly this was not to be.

In August 2018, Beck was able to obtain a search warrant for Marty's house. And this turned out to be a good day for us. Beck called Marty to advise that police would be coming to his house. He didn't answer, but Beck left a message to say they would be attending his home and would enter and search it regardless of whether he was there. When police entered, Marty was not at home, and Beck could hardly believe her eyes when she opened a plastic bag sitting in plain sight on the dining table. In it was a pair of woollen gloves, sticky tape, and a balaclava—all the materials Marty had been using to hide his identity and deliver offensive posters and flyers. And it looked like he was getting ready to attack again. There was a printout with a photo cut out of it, obviously to be used in creating another flyer.

It was a good day, but we weren't quite there yet. Marty had been careful to hide his identity when creating and posting the flyers. When he posted them, he used a postage-paid envelope to avoid licking a stamp and leaving his DNA on the envelope. The envelopes were closed with sticky tape—again, so he didn't leave his DNA behind. He used different printing services to print the

The infamous balaclava

flyers. In fact, he could even claim that he couldn't have made them because he didn't own a computer. But a roll of sticky tape, the gloves Marty wore when he sealed the letters shut and the balaclava he wore to deliver them wasn't enough evidence to convict him. Not without a confession. Beck Norris had to find another way...

In fact, Beck had been pursuing another line of enquiry for some time. Back in June, at around 7 pm on the day Marty had breached his IVO by going to Big W, Beck called and asked me to put her on speaker so both Rhiannon and I could hear what she had to say. I put the phone on speaker as requested, and Beck asked if I had Netflix. I thought this was a strange question. I said I did, and then she told me to watch a Netflix series called *Manhunt: Unabomber*, which was about former FBI agent James R. Fitzgerald and the work he had done with the FBI that helped to catch the Unabomber. There were eight episodes in the series, and I stayed up that night and binge watched the first six of them.

James R. Fitzgerald had used linguistic (language) analysis to help convict the Unabomber. This involves looking for patterns, signals and signs that reveal the identity of an anonymous writer. It can also detect whether different documents have been created by one person. The conviction of the Unabomber was the first time linguistic analysis had been used in a criminal conviction, ending the Unabomber's violent, seventeen-year crime spree. I was astonished to hear that Beck had contacted James R. Fitzgerald for assistance with my case, and even more astonished that he had agreed to help.

Through the course of her investigation, Beck had collected twenty-odd flyers. Unfortunately, some had been thrown out, but she was lucky when a flyer posted on the day of the walk for Karen Chetcuti turned up. She spent some time preparing evidence and a report for James R. Fitzgerald. That evidence included the flyers she had, the love letters Marty had sent me when we were dating, and court documents Marty had prepared. The evidence was duly sent to James R. Fitzgerald for linguistic analysis.

We hoped that bringing in James R. Fitzgerald would lead to a conviction, but it would take time for him to prepare his report. Meanwhile, all the stress had resulted in a bout of shingles and I needed a week off work. And with my birthday approaching, I was waiting for another attack. Another bit of good news came on 24 November, when Rhiannon noticed that Marty had a 'for sale' sign out the front of his house. Good riddance, I thought. I emailed Beck to tell her he was moving. Funny what a search warrant will do.

February came, and one night at around 11.30 pm I thought I heard a police helicopter outside. I was watching TV, and had to keep turning the volume up, thinking the helicopter was very loud and close. I went outside to look; it wasn't there, but I heard it behind me. I turned around, and there was the drone, hovering above my head. I screamed, ran inside, grabbed the home phone to call Triple Zero, then went back outside to film the drone with my mobile. Again, the police didn't attend. My neighbours also came out to see what was going on. They agreed the noise was unbearable.

But February also brought good news. Beck received the linguistic analysis report from James R. Fitzgerald. The purpose of the report was to try to determine whether the flyers left at the Winelarder and other venues were written by the same person who authored the love letters Marty had sent me early in our relationship. Those love letters were signed—they were known communications. The flyers, being unsigned, were questioned communications. James's report compares the two groups of letters and looks for patterns. It's thirteen pages long, but only one sentence mattered: '... it is the opinion of [James R. Fitzgerald] that the writing style found within the [flyers and posters], when compared to the writing style of [the author of the love letters] is **CONSISTENT** to the degree of **Exceptionally Distinctive.**'

In other words, the guy who wrote the love letters also wrote the flyers. Bingo!

IN APRIL 2019, police charged Marty with twenty-eight charges, including stalking, breaking his intervention order, breaching bail, recklessly causing serious injury and intentionally causing serious injury.

The final charge referred to my PTSD, depression and anxiety. I had first been referred to a counsellor by Merri Health way back in 2015 when Marty's attacks were causing terrible insomnia. The treatment included hypnotherapy, but sadly neither that nor the counselling was effective. What I really needed was for the attacks to stop, not just talking therapy. In 2019 I started seeing another psychologist, who formally diagnosed me with depression, anxiety and PTSD, and submitted a report to the courts. I still see her to this day.

We were so close to securing a conviction, but this final leg of the journey would take some time. I was made aware that the court proceedings may last eighteen months. The committal stage, where the evidence would be tested in the Magistrates Court and Marty would enter a plea, could involve up to three hearings. If Marty pleaded not guilty there would be a trial in the County Court. If convicted he could appeal the verdict or the sentence. I'd also been told that, should we go to trial and I had to take the witness stand, the questioning would be brutal. I was beyond scared—actually, petrified—but I knew I had to do it. I just hoped I would be able keep my emotions in check. I didn't need another bout of shingles.

The committal hearing, when we would learn if there would be a trial, was set for 23 and 24 October 2019 at the Melbourne Magistrates Court. I was happy we wouldn't be at Broadmeadows, home of the smirking magistrate. The night before, I checked into a favourite city hotel with some friends. It was a tactic designed to settle my nerves and keep my mind occupied with something other than the trial of Marty Norman. It felt good to have a swim, sauna and spa along with a beautiful dinner and amazing company. We had a few champagnes, laughed the night away, and I managed to get some sleep.

I arrived at the prosecutor's office with a group of friends and supporters, including Beck Norris, my daughter Amity, and John—the new man in my life. The prosecutor came in and advised there had been a development. Marty had originally pleaded not guilty, but if found guilty he faced a maximum of fifteen years and three months in jail. We were informed that he had changed his plea to guilty of one charge of stalking out of the twenty-eight charges. Clearly he had done this for a reduced sentence. I was absolutely livid and asked for this to be rejected. To my horror, we couldn't do this. We had to present a counter plea.

I thought this was just crazy. How did Marty think he could get away with pleading guilty to just one charge? I wanted the charge of 'recklessly causing serious injury' left in for the counter plea. The prosecutor said no to this, which I argued against so ferociously that Amity and John could hear my voice from outside the meeting room. The argument I made was that without this charge, the magistrate would not understand how my mental illnesses related to the charge of stalking. I said I was willing to be a test case; I wanted this charge in, as Marty had caused my PTSD, depression and anxiety. I didn't have those issues before I met him, but sadly I do now.

In the end, after a lot of deliberation, we sent a counter plea to Marty's counsel, which consisted of:

- Stalking, which had eighteen sub-charges
- Breaching court orders, which also had eighteen sub-charges
- Offending while on bail

The counter plea was accepted. This meant there would be no trial, I didn't have to take the stand, and there would be no court the next day. It also meant that James R. Fitzgerald, who had been standing by to join proceedings via a video link, would not have to testify. The next step in the process would be a plea hearing, at which both the prosecution and defence would present information to the magistrate to enable him or her to determine the sentence.

The plea hearing was set for 9 December. I was initially relieved that Marty had pleaded guilty, but later wasn't so sure. If I'd been able to take the stand, I'd have been able to have my say.

I WAS ADVISED to write a Victim Impact Statement (VIS) for the plea hearing. This would help the magistrate understand how the experience of stalking had affected me, which was important information for determining Marty's sentence. It was a confronting thing to do, but once I started writing, I couldn't stop. It all came out—everything—including the tragedy of Cathie's death.

I started by saying that I was 'One Tin Soldier'. In other words, I was on my own, as all the previous victims who had been contacted refused to help. Marty had been stalking women since the 1980s, and decades later he was still controlling them through fear.

In my victim impact statement, I talked about how the posting of the flyers affected me and how they were put up on significant dates in my life, such as birthdays, deaths or celebrations. I listed all the security measures I now had at my home, and the difficulty I had in getting help from the police in the beginning. I said I felt like I wasn't doing a good job as a parent, as Marty had attacked Rhiannon twice and had been to jail for it. I also added how naïve I was, thinking that the ten-year intervention order would offer some protection. I had no safety at my workplace, so I had to quit my job and find another after nearly a decade with Big W.

I described the stress I was constantly under, and that I had been diagnosed with PTSD, then depression and anxiety. I described the physical dread I felt every time we had to go to court, how trying to navigate the court system was foreign to me and that I had lost count of how many times I had been to court.

I ended my victim impact statement with a plea to the magistrate...

I'm asking Your Honour that with the sentence you hand down, that you please consider my sanity over this. I have mentioned being diagnosed with PTSD and major depression and I worry for my future, as his crimes were so egregious, emotionally and mentally violent, I believe that as soon as he's released, he will start back up again. The longer his sentence, the longer peace will live within me, otherwise I will never feel at ease, as someone in law enforcement has stated that having a stalker is like

having your own private terrorist, you never know when or how
he is going to strike, please Your Honour, I am begging for your
assistance to give me back my freedom, my life, my peace and
my sanity.

The night before the plea hearing, I once again checked into my favourite hotel in Melbourne in the company of good friends. I felt really blessed to have such amazing friends who stood by me throughout all of this and for nearly five years. John, the new man in my life was there, plus my friends Mandy, Kaz and Robyn, and my darling Aunty Wilma. These people put up with the tears and the tantrums, and were sometimes victims as well. But we survived. I'm a little different, but I'm still here. I'm still here to tell my story, when it could have been so very different.

That night, I was feeling empowered, knowing that Marty was looking at jail time. The charges he was facing carried a maximum sentence of fifteen years and three months. I expected it would be at least three years and at best five years. I was praying to all the gods and all the spirits to help me finally receive the justice I deserved. The courtroom the next day was going to be filled with everyone who, over the years, had attended court with me. Such a momentous occasion; I was so looking forward to it...

The next day I arrived at Melbourne Magistrates Court and met my legal team out the front of our assigned courtroom. This time I had a new prosecutor, David, who told me that Marty and his barrister had a copy of my victim impact statement and were going through it in case they needed to omit any of it. What!!! *Omit* any of it? Marty could censor my statement? Really? I felt like Marty could suppress any part he found unacceptable, anything he found offensive. I was astounded that he could do that to MY victim impact statement. If he didn't like what I'd written, maybe he should have left me the f**k alone.

I received my statement back and sure enough, it had been censored. Perhaps I didn't fully understand this at the time, but victim impact statements are technically evidence, and as such have to meet certain criteria to be admissible. I had found the guidelines for writing my VIS very restrictive, and essentially ignored them. This may have led to what I felt was censorship, but to me it seemed Marty couldn't handle the truth in black and white. I was furious that I couldn't read out certain parts of my statement. All of the redacted parts were about Cathie, and how I felt threatened and in fear of my life.

In the courtroom, Marty's barrister read out the submissions before the magistrate, and the prosecutor read out the charges and what was involved with all of them. I was then asked to read out my victim impact statement. I took the stand but not the witness box; I chose to stand where the prosecutor and barrister stand when they are addressing the magistrate. I placed my statement down and began to read it to the court. I was shocked by the sound of my voice, which was shaking and quivering. I had never read the statement aloud before, because whenever I tried to practise it I would start to cry. But this time I would have to get through all of it.

While I was reading my statement, I glanced over at the magistrate, who had a paper copy but seemed to have trouble following what I was reading. Clearly, he had the full version and did not know that the statement had been censored.

It took me twenty minutes to read all the way through my statement, and at one point I had to ask Lana, a solicitor with the prosecutor's office, to take over because I couldn't control my tears. Afterwards I sat down with Beck, who gave me a cuddle and said, 'Well done.'

The magistrate then advised us that Marty had written his own character reference—yes, I kid you not. I was shocked, and I looked at Beck, asking, 'Can Marty do this?' Apparently he could, but it was evidence of his narcissism. However, Marty apparently didn't have the guts to read his statement, so his barrister stepped in. I don't recall much about what was in Marty's statement, but the magistrate listened carefully. He picked up the fact that that in the statement Marty expressed no emotion, showed no remorse for his actions, and apologised only to his family. The magistrate asked Marty, 'Where is the apology to Dianne McDonald? Where is the remorse for Dianne McDonald?'

Nothing, zip, silence. Marty just sat there looking ahead, saying nothing. The magistrate also noted that Marty only pleaded guilty at the last minute, at the committal hearing, with the hope of a shorter sentence. After making these comments, the magistrate stated that he was going to have a five-minute break to read through Marty's psychologist's report.

He took a lot longer than five minutes. When he came back into the courtroom the magistrate said he didn't understand the psychologist's report, as it seemed to have some contradictions. He had to Google the illnesses mentioned, and said the report made no sense, as one of the illnesses implied that Marty was doing all of this out of love for me. Clearly it was not love Marty was showing me, but anger and violence. The magistrate also stated that the report looked badly written, unlike the report from my psychologist.

The magistrate then requested that further investigation be undertaken into Marty's mental health report. They would have to go directly to his psychologist for clarification. At this point, court was adjourned until Wednesday 11 December. The magistrate then advised Marty to make sure he showed up at court and also told him to bring a toothbrush. It sounded like Marty was going to jail.

We were back two days later as instructed, only to have the hearing adjourned again until 19 February to further clarify Marty's psych report. When Marty was charged, I thought the end was in sight. But on and on and on the court merry-go-round went. The endless adjournments and delays were just adding to the damage that Marty's stalking had done.

I HAD MET Marty in late 2014. It was now early 2020 — over five years later I was still trying to put an end to the madness and havoc this man had created in my life.

Sadly, 2020 didn't begin well for the east coast of Australia, with massive bushfires everywhere. The loss and devastation was heartbreaking. So much wildlife was destroyed and so many people lost their homes. On the news I saw people taking the shirts off their back to wrap around burnt koalas and giving them water from bottles.

I had my own hard times to deal with in early 2020, beyond the stress Marty was causing. I had kept everything that was happening with Marty from my mother, who had been in a nursing home since 2016. Aside from the first attack on her home, which occurred when she was still living there, she had no idea what was going on.

By this time we had moved Mum out of her original nursing home and into a lovely new one. They had silver service for the residents and their families on Sundays, and served a three-course meal complete with wine. Mum was in heaven—until we started getting calls from the home. They said Mum was becoming stubborn, not wanting to join in, not eating, and not getting up to go to the toilet. She was deteriorating very quickly, to the point where the staff said Mum needed high care. We moved her to another home in the same suburb, but she continued to deteriorate.

One night, the home called to advise they had called an ambulance for Mum, and she had been taken to the Austin Hospital. The hospital called again at 3am and asked me to come in straight away. I called Michelle, and met her at the hospital. A doctor came and asked us about end-of-life care for Mum. We agreed that it was time to let her go, and Mum was returned to her nursing home with medication to make her comfortable.

She passed away at 11 pm on 11 February.

UNDER NORMAL CIRCUMSTANCES, I would have been able to grieve for my mother in peace. But I had to put that important emotional work to one side—I had to go to court on 19 February.

Again, I booked into a hotel the night before the hearing and had the company of close friends.

In the morning, we headed into the courtroom to hear about Marty's psych report. The magistrate began by saying he had read and re-read my victim impact statement, and he agreed with me that I would be in serious danger once Marty was released from jail. The magistrate was going to implement a community corrections order as well as jail time for Marty. Court was then adjourned again. They wanted us to come back on the Friday for the sentencing, but I explained that was the day of Mum's funeral so we adjourned until the next day.

The endless adjournments continued to frustrate me, and the bad news kept coming. It was then that the prosecutor advised me that regardless of the sentence Marty received, he would get a 'credit' for time already served when he went to jail for stalking Rhiannon. WTF? I was furious. He would receive a one-month credit, which meant if Marty received a one-year sentence, it would be eleven months with a community corrections order upon release. I felt like the legal system is for the welfare of the criminals, not the victims. How could Marty receive a credit from a different case on a different matter? Apparently, because it was the same crime. Because he'd been found guilty of stalking us both, he got a reduced sentence. It wouldn't matter if Rhiannon wasn't my daughter. Even if she were a complete stranger and Marty had gone to jail for stalking her, the one-month credit would apply. If he was convicted for stalking someone else in the future, any sentence he received would be shortened through the credit earned when he went to jail for stalking me. Ludicrous...

On 20 February, we all went into the courtroom at 2 pm to hear what the sentence would be. The magistrate handed down an eight-month jail term, followed by a two-year community corrections order. Marty had given me a five-year sentence with no bail, no protection, no nothing. And all he got in return was eight lousy months out of a possible fifteen years and three months. My expectations had been way off.

I felt let down by this lenient sentence. Marty had shown no leniency when he was stalking me. I was also advised that Marty would probably go into protective custody, as he would be seen as a weak prisoner and an easy target. Again, why wasn't I able to get protection from the law when Marty was stalking me? These thoughts soured what should have felt like a moment of triumph.

After the sentence was handed down, Marty's barrister immediately put in a request to appeal the sentence. This meant we had to wait around at the court until almost 5 pm, when the appeal hearing was granted. Marty was to be released on appeals bail and the magistrate handed down the bail conditions, but Marty didn't like them. He instructed his barrister to reduce the number of days he had to report to his local police station each week. The magistrate declined to grant this request, and said Marty would now have to report on Mondays, Wednesdays and Fridays—one more day than the original conditions.

While this discussion took place I could see Marty standing behind the glass walls of the dock with two prison guards. He was fuming. He said the magistrate had the days wrong and he was only supposed to report one day a week. An argument with the magistrate ensued, which Marty lost. Marty then turned to his barrister and shot her the filthiest look; he hadn't gotten his way and looked like he was ready to kill her. At last I started to feel lighter. In fact I started to laugh. I had to stifle my laughter—God forbid the magistrate see me—but Marty saw me and my mirth infuriated him further. A small win, but a win nonetheless...

The next day was my mother's funeral, which was emotional and exhausting. This was a horrific time for me. You expect your mother's funeral to be a sad occasion, but on top of my grief I was on high alert, always looking out to see if Marty—who was out on bail—was going to make an unwelcome appearance. Thankfully, he kept away. After getting home that evening, I collapsed with exhaustion.

AS OUR COURT date for the appeal in May approached, Covid-19 began its march across the globe from Wuhan in China and it wasn't long before we felt the effects in Australia. In March, our head office in the Netherlands advised that we would be moving to work from home, and 17 March was my last day in the office. I was lucky that we had a smooth transition and grateful that I was still working and not on any government payment.

Soon we were all in lockdown. I wondered how this would affect our court date. On 6 May, Beck emailed me to advise that the court date had been adjourned until 2 June—not because of Covid, but because Marty was having yet another psych assessment. This time it was from a place called Spectrum, a centre that dealt with people with personality disorders. I wasn't sure why he needed an assessment, as we already knew he was a diagnosed narcissist. When he had been in the family court in Brisbane, Marty had a court-ordered evaluation, which we had obtained, that made the diagnosis. Now he was doctor-shopping in an effort to go through the system as a mental health inmate so that he wouldn't be placed in the general population in jail. Again, Marty was controlling the situation, controlling the courts, wasting time... I was beyond upset; it seemed like it was never going to end.

I didn't sleep for days after this latest delay. I was so close to it all being over, then whoosh—the finish line was moved again. I had to keep going, but when did any of this become about me? Why was it still about Marty and his needs? His wellbeing? Where was the concern for me? And all this for a lousy eight months in jail.

Where was my justice? I wanted my best friend back; she was attacked as much as I was. It was so unfair. It seemed that crime really does pay, and that having no conscience, and being a liar and one hell of an actor gets you what you want in this world. Being a good, law-abiding person and being kind to others gets you nothing. I wished I could go back in time. I needed a DeLorean. I also needed Doc and Michael J. to drive it and take me back to a time before this nightmare had begun.

My head was not in a good place...

I DIDN'T THINK I'd be able to attend the appeals hearing due to Covid restrictions but, the day before, we were told we could be present. Yay! After three months in lockdown, for me, this was a small win. To be there and see him taken away in handcuffs, oh the shame...

I got a bit emotional when I arrived at the court. Despite longing for this day for years, it was a big change in my life and I was having a hard time with change. Among other things, I was sad that I might never see Beck again; I had come to rely on her the same way I relied on Cathie. I would email Beck with any stupid thought I had in my head, but now this would be gone.

Soon Marty arrived with his barrister. He walked with confidence, and went straight into the court. My supporters—Aunty Wilma and Mandy—and I followed once we knew he had gone through the security check and we wouldn't run into him.

The hearing was in the County Court, and was presided over by Judge Martine Mariach. Marty's barrister started by reading her submissions, and then went through the paperwork with the judge.

Next it was David's turn to speak. He went through all the charges and stated that the victim—that is, me—was in the courtroom. Judge Mariach stopped David and directed a question to me. She asked me what I wanted to be known as during the proceedings. I preferred the term 'Victim' rather than 'Complainant'—Marty had to face what he had done to me and I wanted it known how

A much-needed hug from Beck

I felt. David continued reading out all the charges and listing the evidence.

David then read the contents of all the flyers, one by one. He explained the effect that posting flyers had on me, and the effect that Marty was hoping to cause. He wanted to defame me, to shame me, and ultimately cause me physical pain. Listening to David read out all the flyers like this, one by one, and hear him summarise Marty's insidious intent was quite distressing.

The judge then asked Marty's barrister questions. The barrister began her answers with the comment that Marty had 'yet undiagnosed' mental illnesses. Marty was now claiming to have PTSD, anxiety and depression, which were actually my illnesses. I had learnt that narcissists often project in this way. Marty's barrister explained these illnesses to the judge. Judge Mariach then asked Marty's barrister if all the learned medical people who had previously supplied reports were wrong, was their diagnosis incorrect?

Marty's barrister replied, 'No it wasn't,' and had to admit their diagnosis was, in fact, correct. Judge Mariach was having none of this nonsense. She issued Marty and his barrister a warning—this was what I had been waiting for. Beck looked at me and mouthed that Marty was in trouble. I looked past Beck to where Marty was sitting, and saw that his legs were shaking. Suddenly, the confidence he'd had walking into the courtroom vanished.

Judge Mariach asked the barrister to take Marty outside, find a room, and talk about his options, as she was considering increasing Marty's sentence. I went outside with Mandy and Aunty Wilma to wait.

Twenty minutes later we were back in the courtroom, where Marty's barrister announced very quietly that they were abandoning the appeal. The original sentence from February would stand, effective immediately. Marty's barrister said this so quietly that Beck and I missed it. Suddenly the judge was leaving and the clerk was announcing that court was adjourned until the next day. I asked Beck if we had to come back, but David stepped in to tell us that Marty had abandoned the appeal. He was off to jail.

We went outside, debriefing and congratulating each other. Our hard work had finally paid off. Yes, a longer sentence would have been better, but given the times we now lived in with COVID-19, we were just lucky he was still going to jail. Covid was causing problems in jails, where the crowded conditions could cause it to spread quickly. There had been calls to release prisoners early, reduce sentences and sometimes not send prisoners to jail at all. In fact I believe all this talk in the media was why Marty had looked so confident walking into court to hear his sentence—he thought he'd get out of going to jail altogether.

Outside, we were approached by a prison officer and asked to move to a seating area out of sight because the prisoner was refusing to leave while we were out there. I said to Beck, 'Are you kidding?' Marty was still trying to control things. Everyone obeyed the prison officer's request, but Beck and I stood just outside the seating area and watched Marty's walk of shame. He was hand-cuffed and wearing a face mask, bright blue latex gloves and booties. It was a sight to behold. Finally, HE WAS GOING TO JAIL...

PART 2

PARLIAMENT, PODCASTS AND PEACE

CHAPTER 8

LOCKED UP AND LOCKED DOWN

MARTY NORMAN WAS led out of the dock in handcuffs to begin his jail sentence on 2 June 2020. At that stage Victoria was enjoying the easing of Covid lockdown restrictions that had been introduced on 31 March.

I had spent the last five years unable to move freely about Melbourne without fearing for my safety. I was looking forward to going out and not having to worry about my car, my house, my friends and my family while he was in jail. The hunger I had to live my life in freedom and peace—to go out and see bands, or visit friends, or go to the football, or enjoy a drink or meal at a favourite bar or restaurant—was intense.

But my hopes for freedom were short lived; Covid came back. There were seventy-five new infections on 29 June 2020, followed by sixty-four new infections on 30 June. These numbers were concentrated in Melbourne's north west, and a 'post code' lockdown was announced. Approximately 311,000 people were required to stay at home across thirty-six suburbs, and Craigieburn was one of them. A week later, the whole of Melbourne was back in a lockdown that would last 111 days. This lockdown was stricter than the first. Retail stores were closed, we could not travel more than five kilometres from home, and a curfew was in place between 8 pm and 5 am.

I spent all day, every day, in my house. The company I worked for had moved to remote working, but that didn't mean things were quiet. In fact we were incredibly busy and I was doing a lot of overtime. We had a high turnover and I was also training new staff over the internet. I was working twelve-hour days, and often unable to even pursue permitted activities like shopping or that crucial daily hour of outdoor exercise. My life became a pit of self-pity, and I was barely keeping things together. I may as well have been in jail myself. And to make matters worse, Marty's jail sentence was shrinking.

When the perpetrator of a crime against you goes to jail, you're asked if you'd like to be on the Victims Register. I had been put on the Register when Marty went to jail for stalking Rhiannon, and when he went to jail for a second time I thought I was still on the Register. But I wasn't. I had to re-register when Marty was imprisoned again, as he had completed the first sentence and his file was closed. This may sound like a pretty minor bit of life admin, but I had been traumatised by Marty's stalking and every time I had to think about him or take some action it added to the damage and slowed any healing I had managed to achieve.

What was even worse was that the Victims Register started sending me emails every couple of weeks to advise of a new release date for Marty. What the ... ? They didn't even have the decency to call me personally and give me an explanation, which I found very cruel. I rang the Register to find out what was going on, and it turned out that Marty's sentence was being reduced because he had been credited with 'Emergency Management Days'.

Emergency Management Day credits were awarded to prisoners to compensate for the extra restrictions imposed upon them to prevent the spread of Covid in jails. These restrictions included fewer hours out of cells and being placed in fourteen-day quarantine regardless of infection risk. A law was passed that allowed up to four days to be taken off a prisoner's sentence for every day they were subjected to these extra restrictions. The state government was only crediting prisoners with one day per day of lockdown to reflect the impact of the pandemic on the wider community, but this was cold comfort for me as I watched Marty's sentence shrink and the threat of him reoffending come closer and closer.

It got to the point that Marty had twenty-two days taken off his jail time. This was ridiculous—soon there'd be nothing left of his sentence. I called Ed O'Donohue, the Shadow Attorney General, to ask what he could do to have these credits removed or revoked so that Marty would serve the entire sentence, or at the very least have no more credits added. I have to say I was a bit angry, pretty pissed off, and more than annoyed that this was happening. Poor Ed bore the brunt of all of my emotions on that call. But everything seemed to be going Marty's way. I felt like his welfare and his human rights were better protected than mine.

Ed contacted the Corrections Minister, Natalie Hutchins, who advised that she wouldn't revoke the twenty-two days but would have no more added. I guess that was better than nothing, but it was small comfort. Marty's new release date was 10 January 2021.

It seemed insane that after I had finally got Marty into jail, I had to fight to keep him there because of a lockdown that made *me* feel like I was in jail. I was discovering that convicting and jailing the perpetrator of a crime does not mark the end of the victim's suffering.

BACK IN APRIL 2020, electronic monitoring had become available in Victoria for magistrates to implement upon sentencing. Because Marty was sentenced in February, it could not be part of his community corrections order (CCO) I wasn't aware of the change to the law at the time, but when I learnt about it in December that year I made efforts to vary the CCO on Marty to include electronic monitoring.

Again, I went to Ed O'Donohue for help and was referred to the Attorney General. Jill Hennessy was the Attorney General at the time, and Ed wrote to her on my behalf. On 16 December Ed received a disappointing reply. The letter advised me to call Triple Zero if I felt like I was in danger. I found this suggestion condescending—I had lost count of how many times I had called Triple Zero. It also stated that to have the CCO varied, Marty would have to re-offend or conduct vexatious proceedings against me. Jill did acknowledge and sympathise with my situation, and contacted the Department of Justice and Community Safety to urgently review my case and contact me to discuss the matter in further detail. But I have to say that I was disappointed in the outcome.

I also contacted our state premier, Daniel Andrews, and the letter I received just referred me back to Jill Hennessy and Lisa Neville, the Minister for Police. This was particularly frustrating as the premier had referred to my case in a press conference and implied that it would be easy to add electronic monitoring to the CCO. It felt like I was going around in circles and had exhausted all avenues to obtain a hearing to vary the CCO. I was feeling pretty angry at having hit another dead end.

My lawyer, Peter, then contacted the Department of Justice and Community Safety. Again, we were given the run around. They said the use of electronic monitoring was ultimately determined by the magistrate at the time of sentencing the conditions of a community corrections order. They also explained that, given the restrictive nature of electronic monitoring, it must only be considered if the offender is at great risk of reoffending. If the offender reoffended, then electronic monitoring would be proportionate and justified. In other words, Marty would have to stalk me again before we could add measures that would stop him from stalking me again. Oh, the irony. I found the letter hugely offensive—we could only react to Marty instead of being proactive to prevent any reoffending. I felt that Marty's needs and comfort were being put ahead of mine.

I HAD SUFFERED in many ways—emotionally and psychologically, but also financially. Compensation is available through Victims of Crime, and I had made an application in November 2015. Nine months later, in August 2016, I learnt that the hearing for my case would not go ahead and had been struck out. VOC (Victims of Crime) didn't see the need for all the security measures I had put in my home. Apparently, if it had been at work that I needed help, that would have been another matter.

Months later—in February 2018—I tried again. I met Rachel Carling-Jenkins MP at a rally at Parliament House organised by Protect Victoria, and she offered to look into the matter for me. I ended up spending an hour with Rachel and her head of staff advising on what I believed

were the flaws with intervention orders and what needed
to change. When I received a second intervention order
against Marty, none of the convictions from the first
order carried over, so he started with a clean slate. Most
orders are only for one year, but with my second order
being for ten years I at least had some protection that
everything he did to me would be listed.

I was also upset about being called 'an affected family
member'. I never lived with Marty, never married him,
never had children with him, so how did I come under
that banner? The problem was that I didn't slot neatly
into any category, and that was the closest they could put
me in. But this generic phrasing disgusted me. It made
my stomach churn, having people think I was related to
Marty in any way or had a domestic relationship with
him. The same went for Rhiannon; she was not his daughter. I said this needed to change; they needed to create
a category for people who had only dated. We need
terminology that encompasses all genders, all relationships and all situations. Having a stalker is like having a
private terrorist. I'd like to see the term 'personal terror-
ism' introduced to the legal context.

Rachel looked through my file, which was extensive,
and couldn't believe my case had been thrown out. She
promised to organise a tribunal hearing for me to have
my case heard again. I remember driving home after
that meeting in awful peak hour traffic, but it was worth
it. My meeting with Rachel was one of the few times
when I was being stalked by Marty that I felt somewhat
empowered.

The new hearing was slated for 11 May 2018 at Broadmeadows Court, and I attended with my lawyer at the
time, Luke. When the magistrate came out, I was horrified; I knew things would not be going my way. It was

the same magistrate who gave Marty the order on me based on false documents. Needless to say, he denied my application, told me to come back when I had a case, and smirked at me again. Later I received a letter from Victims of Crime (VOC) saying they were keeping my file open to resubmit with the police briefs, paperwork from the previous hearing and any submissions for acts of violence. But I decided not to worry about VOC any time soon.

In 2020, when Marty was in jail, I reapplied for Victims of Crime compensation after my new lawyer, Peter, gave me the name of a friend who could help me with this. My previous lawyer, Luke, had become a barrister and was no longer able to represent me, but finding Peter was a bright spot in my story. I'd been on the train, talking to my 'train buddies', Kaz and Nishty, and Peter overheard my conversation. He knew Kaz, gave her his card and said he'd be able to help me.

I started my application for the final time on 31 July 2020. It's such a long process, and I was only claiming for my medical bills and security for my home and my car. I wasn't claiming for loss of income as I was using annual leave or sick leave to go to court or appointments. I had a lot of appointments: with my dentist to fix my teeth; with my original psychologist for counselling for PTSD, depression and anxiety; with my hairdresser to deal with the fact that my hair had turned white and was falling out; with my doctor to get pain medication for my hip, as the stress would go straight to that part of my body and stop me in my tracks. I also had to pay for these doctors and specialists. At this point I had used around $45,000 from the equity in my home and was hopeful I would get a good outcome from Victims of Crime.

I was eventually awarded $12,965. This was much better than having my case thrown out by a smirking magistrate, but not only was it inadequate financially, it didn't represent compensation for the suffering and mental illness I have experienced as a result of being stalked. There is more work to do here. And by this time I had— perhaps unintentionally and certainly not in a planned way—started to become an advocate not just for myself, but for other victims of stalking.

AT THE BEGINNING of 2018 I had decided I would give myself some downtime that year. When Cathie passed away, I was contacted by a friend of hers named Katie, who ran an art class at a wine bar on Wednesdays after work. I thought, why not? It might provide an oasis of comfort in my anxiety-riddled life. At the first class I sat next to a woman named Cheryl, who started asking me questions about a hot story that was in the news. I asked Cheryl where she worked. She said the ABC newsroom. I laughed and said, 'If you want a story, I have one for you,' and started to tell her about my life.

At the next class, Cheryl took a seat next to me when she arrived, and asked if I'd be interested in doing a story for the ABC. I had already approached another TV station twice and been knocked back, so if Cheryl was interested I was going to jump at the chance.

Cheryl and her colleagues at the ABC soon became a fixture in my life. A reporter and cameraman came to the court hearing in 2018 after which Marty went looking for Rhiannon at Big W. A film crew also came to all the court hearings after Marty was charged in early 2019. And of course I had to appear on camera and give reactions to events. At times I found this quite hard, as my emotions were triggered by some of the decisions. But I wanted my story out there and I had to get my emotions under control.

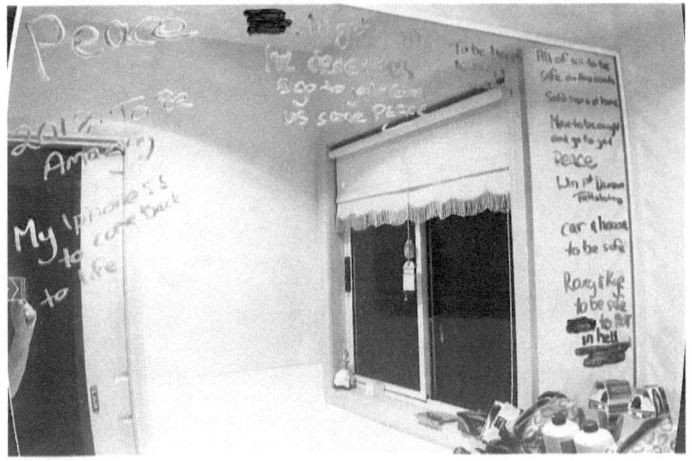

TOP Filming *Australian Story* with the ABC crew

BOTTOM My plea to the universe on my bathroom mirror

Cheryl also wanted to film me at home. I have to admit
I freaked a bit when she told me this. When Marty was
stalking me and I was finding it almost impossible to protect myself, I took some desperate measures—measures
that might look crazy to someone not going through what
I was going through. I had been writing messages on my

With my friend Mandy at the Quill Awards. Sadly, we didn't win

bathroom mirror in lipstick to put my thoughts out into the universe and invite divine intervention. I had started doing this in 2016, after Karen Chetcuti's sister told me about it. I was desperate enough to try anything. The only people who had known about this were Cathie and Rhiannon. Rhiannon thought I'd lost the plot. So when Cheryl said she wanted to come to my home for filming, I had to put a lot of elbow grease into cleaning my bathroom mirror!

The filming Cheryl had been doing was destined for a two-part episode of *Australian Story*. I was looking forward to watching the two episodes while Marty was incarcerated, but the ABC had to fight to have them aired. Marty's lawyer sent a 'cease-and-desist' letter to the ABC after Marty saw a preview of the programme from his jail cell. He was not happy. The ABC decided to air it regardless, as Cheryl had obtained permission at each and every court hearing to use certain content. She had asked for permission to use specific elements of the case, such as police interviews. Each time Cheryl made a request, Marty's barrister replied, 'No objection.' So the cease-and-desist letter had no value.

The first episode of *Australian Story*: 'To Catch a Stalker' aired on 12 October—towards the end of Melbourne's second lockdown. I set up my laptop in the lounge so I could Zoom with my sister and her family while we all watched the show. We had champagne to toast our efforts and the efforts of the ABC in getting the programme on air, despite Marty's efforts to stop it. I hoped the show would get this important subject into the public eye and help people better understand the impact of stalking.

The show was introduced by Debra Newell, whose story of being stalked was immortalised in the Netflix series *Dirty John* and the podcast of the same name. I had found Debra's email address and sent her a message, not thinking for a second that I would get a reply. To my astonishment, her PA, Danielle, wrote back immediately and advised that Debra wanted to be a part of the show. I remember that it was early Sunday morning when I received her email and I was bubbling over with excitement. But it was too early to call anyone with my good news and had to wait and wait before I picked up the phone! Debra is still there for me; she has become someone I call a friend. We are both tied together by an experience few people could really understand.

Enjoying Christmas in peace

Australian Story: 'To Catch a Stalker' proved to be a massive hit for the ABC and the first episode attracted 752,000 viewers. At the time of writing, the first episode also had 888,327 views on YouTube and the second episode had 391,852. And I was delighted when, a few months after it aired, the programme was nominated for four Quill Awards for journalistic excellence. I was amazed at how well received the shows were, and the support I received from the public was nothing short of incredible. I was very humbled by people from all around the world who offered support and thanked me for coming forward and highlighting the insidious crime that is stalking.

Australian Story is seen worldwide, and after it aired I was contacted by a woman from the US called Jaimie, who hosts a podcast with her partner called *Strictly Stalking*. As part of the research for their programme they came across my story. She said they would love to interview me, as they interview stalking victims who have become survivors to show other victims that they can rise above their situation and fight back. This was one of the first times I'd been called a survivor. Beck, and James R. Fitzgerald had called me that, but now everyday people started doing it. It felt surreal, as I didn't see myself that way and things were still very raw.

The idea of appearing on a podcast and talking about my experience was unnerving, and it took me weeks to finally message Jaimie back. I remember that when I did, Marty had exactly eleven days left on his sentence. Those eleven days included Christmas, so at least I was able to enjoy Christmas Day with my sister and her family. I stayed overnight as we celebrated a bit too hard. I can't even remember how many bottles of champagne we had! Marty was due to be released from prison in January. On New Year's Day of 2021, I went out for lunch while I still could without looking over my shoulder.

CHAPTER 9

STAYING STRONG

I HAD A quiet start to 2021 as I prepared for Marty's release on 10 January. I was on high alert, extremely stressed and trying to remember if I actually did have things in place should the worst happen.

I had been regularly speaking with Sergeant Nick De Ridder from Broadmeadows police about all my fears, and he was also concerned about Marty's upcoming release. He told me he was going to send two police officers to remind Marty of what the community corrections order entailed and what the ramifications would be should he breach this order. Marty was told in no uncertain terms to stay away from me, and any of my family or friends, and that the authorities would be watching. The prison also gave Marty an assessment to see how likely he would be to re-offend.

Ed O'Donohue and Glenn Corey were also understandably concerned about the security of their premises, and contacted the sergeant at the local police station to keep him in the loop. Sergeant Mathison then contacted me and was kind enough to give me his mobile number so I could call him directly if there was any trouble.

Another precaution I had in place was a safety watch. After *Australian Story* aired, I was offered the watch by the StandbyU Foundation in Queensland. The watch has a button that the wearer can push if they feel like they're in danger, which sends a call out to five selected friends and family members who can hear what is happening to the person wearing the watch and call for help if necessary. The watch also provides the wearer's location and records for ten minutes after the button is pushed. It's an amazing piece of technology that I was grateful for. My daughter Amity decided to repay StandbyU for their generosity and became a foundation fundraiser for them.

As Marty's release date came closer, I felt well prepared. In fact I don't think we could have been any more prepared for an attack. I hoped there wouldn't be one, but wasn't convinced that Marty would leave me alone and wanted to be prepared for the worst.

The day of Marty's release was quiet, and I had two detectives at my house to make sure I was okay. The next day was Amity's twenty-fifth birthday. In the past Marty had attacked on significant dates like these, so I was perhaps more worried than I'd been the day before. Happily, nothing happened, and we were able to go out and have a lovely lunch for Amity.

These were anxious times, but I knew I had to be strong. Before Christmas, my children had been in touch with 'FBI Jim' as we all now called James R. Fitzgerald. They had requested copies of all his books for me as Christmas presents. They duly arrived on 13 January— albeit a bit late—and I was delighted to see that Jim had signed and left messages for me inside each and every one of them. He also included a card with a very special and empowering message for me. It said:

'Dianne,

I've coined a new term. It's "Dianne-Strong" It applies perfectly to you. You're a hero! Stay strong.'

I HAD THIS framed, so when I'm down and thinking, 'I can't do this,' I read Jim's message and know I can as I've been through worse. FBI Jim had faith in my ability to help other victims and survivors of stalking, so how could I not keep going?

Opportunities to help stalking victims had already started to come my way. Jaimie and Jake from the *Strictly Stalking* podcast had confirmed they wanted to do an episode with me. After listening to many of their podcasts, I discovered that these stalking cases had one thing in common—they all involved coercive control. No matter what the relationship was between the stalker and their prey, it always involved some kind of control.

Jaimie and Jake sent through a list of questions and I had my first Zoom meeting with them on 22 January. A week later we recorded the podcast. The recording seemed to go well, but on reflection, I was very green. I had not done a podcast before, let alone a podcast produced in another country. Sometimes the language didn't translate; for example I would say 'intervention' order instead of 'restraining' order. So I think some facts got lost. Listening back to it now, I feel I could have explained myself a bit better. But like I said, I was green and very nervous.

Around this time my teacher from the art classes I'd been going to had an exhibition. At the cocktail party afterwards, I was introduced to a few people who had seen *Australian Story* and knew who I was. And then

Miccy's freshly painted Archibald portrait of me, on the easel
and waiting to be packed and sent to the judging committee

Miccy and Katie, who hosted the class, started whis-
pering in each other's ears and casting me strange
looks. What on earth was going on? Then Katie said to
Miccy, 'Ask her. Go on, ask her.' To my astonishment, Mic
asked if I would sit for him so he could paint my portrait
and enter it in the Archibald Prize. The Archibald was

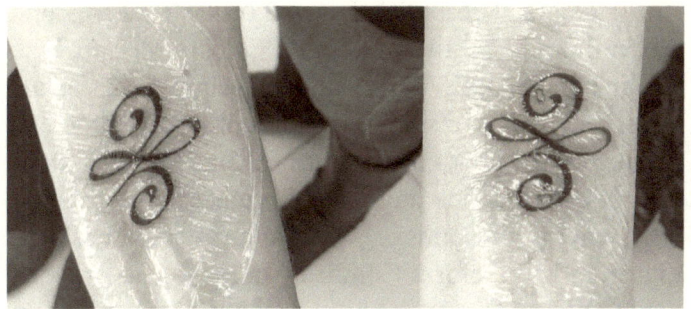

The Shazam Twins' new tattoos

initiated in 1921, and is considered the most prestigious art prize in Australia. Of course I promptly said yes, and went for many sittings at the gallery. The finished portrait was duly sent to the Archibald committee, and we began a nervous five-week wait for the decision.

Meanwhile, Katie and I got to talking about the portrait and also about Cathie. We remembered that Cath was going to get a tattoo of a Celtic symbol for new beginnings. We decided that we would both get that tattoo, and get it on our left wrists as Cathie was left-handed. Today, we touch our left wrists together every time we meet and Katie calls us the 'Shazam' twins. I'm sure people who see this think it's crazy, and maybe it sounds stupid, but it's our way of remembering our dear friend.

Sadly, Miccy's portrait of me didn't win the Archibald Prize. Miccy kindly gave me the painting and today it hangs proudly in my study, where it makes the perfect background for video calls.

RAISING AWARENESS about stalking is important, but what we really need is law reform. In December 2020, Justice Party MP Tania Maxwell tabled a petition in the Victorian Parliament calling for tougher laws to deal with stalkers. The petition had 8,000 signatures and was prompted by the murder of Celeste Manno, who was stabbed to death by her stalker—with whom she had never had a relationship—as she slept in her home in a north-eastern suburb of Melbourne. Tania Maxwell, along with Celeste Manno's mother and brother met with Attorney General Jill Hennessy, who said she would ask the Victorian Law Reform Commission (VLRC) to urgently review Victoria's responses to stalking and harassment.

I contacted the VLRC directly near the closing date for submissions, and spoke to a woman named Marie Barnard. I found out they actually knew about my case, and agreed to wait for my submission. That's how I found myself working with Tania in March 2021, preparing a submission into stalking-law reform for the VLRC.

In May, Tania also put forward a motion in Parliament to reform the Victims of Crime Assistance Act, which was twenty-five years old. I attended a press conference with Tania to discuss how difficult it is to navigate the process of obtaining compensation, and how the slow and complex application actually retraumatises victims. Again, my nerves set in and I rambled about things to the media and spoke for what seemed like forever. Those poor reporters… But Tania's motion was unanimously accepted. It was a start, I thought.

While speaking in Parliament about victims of crime, Tania also brought up my situation when I was in court and had my victim impact statement censored by the perpetrator and his legal team. 'How in God's name can that happen?' Tania asked the Parliament. She was saying that our legal system is not designed to help victims, but rather hinders them. Just after Tania's reform motion was accepted in Parliament, Melbourne was plunged back into a fourteen-day lockdown.

Facing the press with Tania Maxwell (right)

AFTER LOCKDOWN four ended, *The Age* newspaper reached out for an interview. The interview was about what it's like to survive a stalker, how I wanted electronic monitoring as part of the community corrections order on Marty, and my submission on stalking to the VLRC. The article appeared on 25 June with the headline 'I have a jail that he's created in my head'. It quoted some of my submission to the inquiry, which included 'for victims to be believed'. I went on to say I was telling my story over and over again to a new policeman every time I had to report something new that Marty had done. It was frustrating and time consuming, as I'd be in the police station for hours. I told them all I wanted was to be believed—that all these random attacks were actually happening, and they were being perpetrated by the person that I—the victim—said was doing it. It seemed all Marty had to do was deny he was stalking me when police questioned him, and they believed him every time.

I had done a press release on electronic monitoring with the ABC back in January, and around this time I did a follow-up interview with them. The article was written by Cheryl Hall and Belinda Hawkins, who were involved in my *Australian Story* episodes. It discussed electronic monitoring, and featured comments from Tony North QC, who was a former Federal Court judge and chairman of the VLRC. He said:

> ... *electronic monitoring was only done in very few cases in Victoria at the moment, and only after sentencing... The new proposal would allow the electronic monitoring of someone before any conviction... It would be a very dramatic change, but if we were able to design an instrument that measured risk adequately enough then, would it be a good idea?*

Stalking expert Professor Heather Douglas, from The University of Melbourne, also contributed to the article. She said:

> *Certainly in Di McDonald's context, if we had different risk assessment tools, we might have got to the right end-point, which was the prosecution of stalking, at a sooner point in time. Stalking is right up there in the top three or four factors for future domestic violence and harm. It is associated with homicide, and those obsessive behaviours that underpin stalking are much connected to coercive control behaviours.*

I also appeared on an ABC News report in regard to the VLRC enquiry into stalking laws, and electronic monitoring and how it was rejected for Marty. I pointed out the irony that Marty could not be monitored, but at least I was lucky enough to be able to arm myself with electronic monitoring in the form of my safety watch. I was starting to get used to talking to the media, and I was proud of this interview.

After enduring yet another lockdown—this time for twelve days—I had a meeting with the VLRC on 30 July. They had asked me to come in and discuss my experience of stalking in person. I talked about what is lacking when a victim first goes to the police for assistance, and then how abominable the court system is for a first-time user who is completely on their own.

The meeting included Marie Bernard and retired Federal Court Judge Anthony North QC and went for three and a half hours. Afterwards I was exhausted and completely drained—but hopeful about what would come out of this. I made it clear that I was advocating for the criminalisation of coercive control, and they agreed with my thoughts and perceptions. I felt hopeful about what they would eventually submit to the Attorney General and what she in turn would present to Parliament. Fingers crossed this will lead to real change, as it's time...

On 10 August 2021, I finally completed my written submission to the VLRC—it came to 8,982 words. The Commission had a list of thirty questions to consider, and I answered some of them in my submission. I also gave an overview on what police and courts need to do going forward and what it is that victims require. I can only advise the powers that be and hope they will be heard in Parliament, but if we don't use our voices for change, then nothing will change.

As someone with personal experience of stalking, I had clear ideas about what needed to change. The following is an overview of the changes I recommended to the VLRC in my submission:

- Police to believe a victim's account of their stalking when they report it.

- Police to be more thorough when checking what an accused offender is saying. In my case, had police checked Marty's statements, things may have finished in 2016.

- Courts to ask for more evidence to support intervention order applications, and for police statements or other evidence to be attached to the interim order for an order to be granted. I worked hard to prove my case, and yet Marty took me to court based on hearsay and falsified evidence.

- Coercive control to be made a criminal offence.

- Perpetrators not to be given a copy of Victim Impact Statements. This is an insult to a victim.

- To have one officer allocated to you so you don't have to endlessly repeat your story to different people.

- Once a perpetrator has pleaded guilty, there should be no further adjournments to court proceedings. I endured eleven hearings.

- A perpetrator to lose the right to abandon an appeal if they believe it will lead to an increase in their sentence.

- The abolition of Emergency Management Days.

Not long after I made my submission to the VLRC'S enquiry into stalking laws, Melbourne found itself back in lockdown. This time, we were 'incarcerated' for seventy-seven days. Incarcerated is a strong word, but I had felt like I was in jail for almost seven years now, and just wanted to be free. I wished these lockdowns would go away. I'd been going through so much, and I couldn't even see my own family. During this time, I missed both Sam and Rhiannon's birthdays. The one good thing was that Marty was also living in these conditions and couldn't travel to Craigieburn. At least I knew my house and children were safe.

Meanwhile I continued to advocate for stalking victims. The Victorian Government was conducting an inquiry into Victoria's criminal justice system, and asked members of the public to make submissions. I had a parliamentary meeting in regard to this and was speaking via Zoom on 21 September. I put up the link on Facebook so my family and friends could watch. The meeting was chaired by Fiona Patten, leader of the Reason Australia party, and Tania Maxwell, and went very well. I spoke about my story and the changes I think need to be made. I wanted to focus on other things besides stalking, and spoke about coercive control and what I call revenge intervention orders—when the perpetrator applies for an order against you using false documents and accusations. Marty did this to me twice—once using hearsay and once with a fake Facebook post; he had no police reports or witnesses or concrete evidence. The MPs present were shocked that such a practice existed.

It was in this meeting that I said for the first time that having a stalker is like having your own private terrorist. You know they're going to attack, but you don't know where or when or how they'll attack. You can't be pro-active; you can only react when they strike. They have control, while you live in a state of hyper-vigilance. It makes me think of the motto of the RSL: 'The price of freedom is eternal vigilance.' Living under coercive control is hell and intervention orders aren't really worth the paper they're written on.

I was happy with how I was received for this meeting, and my friends left messages on Facebook congratu-lating me for speaking so well under pressure from the barrage of questions I received from the MPs.

A month after this meeting, the lockdown finally ended and Amity, Rhiannon and I were finally able to go out for dinner. It was so wonderful to be able to eat and have a drink together outside our home. It had been forever since we'd been out.

On 4 November, I had a meeting with Fiona McCor-mack, the Victims of Crime Commissioner. The Commis-sioner was conducting a Systemic Inquiry into victim participation in the Justice System. As part of this inquiry, the Commissioner would be looking at victims' experi-ences of participating in the justice system and whether new laws or policies were needed to help victims partic-ipate in keeping with their legal entitlements.

I took many documents with me to show what I'd been through. I wanted to highlight my application for financial assistance from VOC that was struck out, and the experience I had at the tribunal in which a familiar, unsympathetic magistrate smirked at me and told me to come back when I had a case. I also took in court docu-ments, which included my victim impact statement.

The Commissioner was lovely and sympathetic and listened attentively. She even broke down in tears while reading my VIS. I really wasn't sure what to do when this happened, but it showed how much empathy the Commissioner had for victims. She was upset that I had been silenced, that I couldn't say what I wanted to say. She couldn't believe that the offender had control over my VIS, that he had the final say on what I could and couldn't say. The final report to Parliament called to make the system more victim centric and ensure that victims' voices are heard and acted on.

ON 18 NOVEMBER 2021, I received the sad news that Ed O'Donohue was retiring from politics. He'd been in the job for nearly twenty years and had helped so many victims, which is a credit to his career. I watched Ed deliver his final speech in Parliament, and was extremely touched when he mentioned me and another victim and said that helping us were some of his proudest moments. I will be forever grateful to Ed for all his help since 2017; without him, Beck Norris wouldn't be in my life, and I'm sure I'd still be living the stalker nightmare. Ed dealt with a lot of my emotions, the good, the bad and the ugly. He took it all in his stride, and to me that is what you want from Members of Parliament. They are there to help us when we have nowhere else to turn.

Christmas 2021 was a joyous occasion at my sisters'. All of my children were there that year, and it was the first time in six or seven years that we'd all been together for the day. I was looking forward to 2022, and its promise of getting back to normal, seeing friends and family with no restrictions. Melbourne had survived being one of the most locked down cities in the world with a total of 245 days of restrictions. I had survived the experience of being stalked, and since being released from jail Marty Norman had stayed away from me.

BRING ON 2022!

CHAPTER 10

PAYING IT FORWARD

JANUARY 2022 BROUGHT with it a new Covid variant. Omicron had arrived. We couldn't afford to be too complacent and still had restrictions on interstate travel. But it was our health workers I felt incredibly sad for. They were tired and in desperate need of a break. They must have been thinking, what next...

In December of the previous year I had resigned from my corporate job after five and a half years. I knew there would be many people I'd miss, but the whole business of working from home and training new staff had taken a toll. The pressure on me was too much, so I decided to go into the new year with a sense of pride in myself.

As I wasn't working, I started volunteering for Impact, an organisation that supports women and children throughout Victoria to escape extreme violence at home, which was founded by Kathy Kaplan, OAM. Their goal is to offer practical support in meaningful ways to women and children in crisis, while advocating for societal change. I volunteered for shifts at the newly acquired ImpactHouse, where they prepare 'Bags of Love' for women and children in shelters. The bags are filled with toiletries and other essentials, as well as items that bring comfort to the women who receive them. I helped pack up the bags that were sent out for Mother's Day. Another delivery would be sent out at Christmas, and these bags would contain items for children.

It was such an amazing feeling being there and contributing. I felt lucky that I never lived with Marty, or I too could be one of these women needing shelter. I put my name down for several shifts during the week in February, and looked forward to going back there as I was making new friends who were also trying to give back and pay it forward.

Although it had been open for a while, ImpactHouse didn't have their official grand opening until late in March. Fiona Patten MP attended, as well as Assistant Police Commissioner Lauren Callaway. Lauren was overseeing the implementation of a new program call SASH, which stands for Screening Assessment for Stalking and Harassment. In her remarks, Lauren highlighted my case as well as that of Celeste Manno. Too often it is assumed that violence only occurs in domestic situations, but neither myself nor Celeste were in a 'domestic' relationship. Hopefully, SASH will help the authorities more readily identify potentially violent situations.

At this time I was also becoming something of a fixture in Parliament. I was there on 8 March when Tania Maxwell presented amendments to the Victims of Crime Compensation Act. The amendments included having stalking, threats to kill and threats to cause serious injury recognised as crimes. Victims would no longer be told, as I was, to 'come back when they have a case'.

It also implemented legislation that meant an offender would no longer be informed of a victim's compensation claim. In a media statement, Tania said:

> Where a victim seeks help on the path to recovery, the government rightly wanted to prohibit someone who has committed, or is accused of committing, family violence or abhorrent sexual offences from being given notice of the time and place where the hearing is to occur.

Tania went on to explain that while threats to kill, do serious harm and stalking happens within the home and family relationships, these horrific offences also occur beyond it—where people work, socialise and communicate—and they're widely reported as being markers for future violence. Her statement said:

> ... we have a responsibility to provide protection and support for those victims in the same way that we protect victims of family violence. Someone who has a fixation on a person, perhaps without even knowing them personally, can wreak havoc in their victim's life. An opportune offender can use the knowledge of their target's VOCAT [Victims of Crime Assistance Tribunal] hearing to offend again—such as placing a tracking device on the victim or their vehicle. Simply being in the vicinity of the tribunal can become an act of intimidation, alone deterring a victim from even making an application for assistance.

The Bill was supported by the Opposition and voted in unanimously in Parliament. This was such a 'high five' moment for me. I felt like my advocacy was now starting to make a real difference.

The next stop on my advocacy journey was on 24 March, when I once again attended Parliament for the tabling of the Justice System Inquiry that I took part in back in September 2021. One hundred recommendations were put forward. I joined a few other survivors for the tabling, and sincerely thanked Tania Maxwell and Fiona Patten for their tireless work. We celebrated in the gardens in Parliament with a glass of champagne and all spoke at a media conference afterwards.

WHILE KEEPING BUSY with my advocacy work, I'd also been looking for a new job. Around this time I accepted a new position back in retail. Just as I started training in a branch, a customer came up to me and said she recognised me. Then she started crying. My new work colleagues were all wondering what was going on. So I had to tell them my story. My new manager went and watched both episodes of *Australian Story*, then came over and gave me the biggest hug.

I was back in Parliament on 6 April, this time for the tabling of the Interim Stalking Reform Report from the VLRC. I did an interview with ABC News on the steps of Parliament House. I talked about how one police officer should be allocated to look after a victim; a lot of my evidence was lost because multiple officers were involved.

The findings of the interim report found that the police were not taking stalking seriously. Anthony North QC, chair of the VLRC, described stalking as an 'invisible crime' that was frequently not recognised by either the police or the people who experienced it. He stated:

> [Stalking] is often minimised or trivialised, and victim-survivors are often expected to manage the situation on their own. Our recommendations are intended to assist the police to recognise stalking, to take victims seriously, support them, and intervene quickly to stop the stalking.

With fellow advocates Cathy Oddie, Lee Little
and Tracie Oldham, in the library at Parliament

The report stated that the default position for police was to advise victims to apply for a personal safety intervention order (PSIO), which left them feeling like they had to take matters into their own hands. It also called for police to apply for intervention orders on behalf of victims, which is within their power, to improve early responses.

Submissions to the VLRC, including mine, stated that victims felt like they weren't being taken seriously by police, that they were behaving irrationally, and that they were wasting police time. The Commission also heard that victims were sometimes told that taking out an intervention order could compromise their safety, as the stalker can be angered by this and retaliate by increasing their attacks.

The Commission recommended that Victoria Police draw on specialists to provide training to improve front-line police's understanding and identification of stalking. It recommended that the police develop guidelines for specialist interviewing to improve the recording of information to aid investigation of stalking. It also said police officers should provide specific guidance to victims, such as how to end cyberstalking.

Shortly before the interim report was released, Victoria Police announced the trialling of a pilot program that would profile stalkers in an attempt to prevent the behaviour escalating to violence and killings. In an article for *The Guardian*, which I had contributed to, VicPol's family violence assistant commissioner, Lauren Callaway, said the force had 'numerous improvements' underway. She also said:

> *We are the first police jurisdiction in Australia to equip frontline police with an innovative and structured risk assessment tool to better protect victims from unwanted behaviour as part of a trial introduced at Prahran and Morwell police stations last month.*
>
> *These improvements mean we will investigate and respond to these reports swiftly to improve safety for victims and hold perpetrators to account for their harmful actions.*

On 30 June, the final report was tabled. The following is a summary of the recommended changes:

- Providing community education about stalking, and training about stalking for people who work in the justice system

- Providing independent advocates to support people who experience stalking and guide them through every stage of the justice system

- Providing easier access to financial and practical support for people who experience stalking, including technology to fight cyberstalking (such as getting spyware removed from a phone)

- Implementing new protections in the civil and criminal justice system for people who experience stalking

- Reforming the personal safety intervention order (PSIO) system so that stalking cases are prioritised over other, less serious matters

- Building alternative pathways for children and young people who engage in stalking behaviour, to reduce ongoing contact with the justice system

- Ensuring that PSIOS are not made against children under 14

- Making the definition of stalking in the Crimes Act simpler and clearer so that it is easier for police and the courts to apply it

- Improving research and data gathering about stalking and people who stalk

- Providing early intervention to prevent stalking, including treatment and support programs for people who stalk.

I would have liked to be at Parliament House for the tabling of the report, but was at home recovering from hip-replacement surgery. My hip had suffered tremendous deterioration due to the stress I was living with. At this point I was still learning to walk again, and grateful that I had my daughters with me, as I needed their care as rehab was unavailable under ongoing Covid restrictions. So I watched the tabling of the report live online and later received a hard copy. It had eight chapters, and my recommendations and comments were listed in seven of them. My name was also mentioned some twenty-five times. It was a proud moment for me, as it was clear that I had been heard and was able to contribute to real change. I could only hope the recommendations would be implemented quickly.

OPPORTUNITIES TO RAISE awareness about stalking kept coming my way. I filmed a podcast with the Christian and Jewish Council. Mario Bekes, who I was on the podcast with, later approached me to be a guest on his own podcast, called *Life—the Battlefield*. It was empowering to know that people were willing to talk about tough topics so that others can realise that they can survive trauma and get their life back.

Then, just when I was on a high and things seemed to be going in the right direction, I took another hit. On 27 September, Optus, one of Australia's biggest telecommunication companies, announced that they had been hacked and personal information had been leaked. I had previously been a customer with them, but when I changed my phone and phone number I also changed my provider. You would think I was safe, but I wasn't—they had kept my details on file. I felt extremely violated and angry. This breach meant I would have to replace my driver licence as the number has been corrupted. Adding insult to injury, Optus didn't contact me—I had to hear about the breach via a TV news report.

This incident triggered all my old fears, which had been gradually subsiding. I raced into VicRoads to replace my licence. They said they couldn't help until I had filled in an online report via a page that had been set up specifically for Optus customers. Any well-adjusted person would have taken care of that first. But I was beyond stressed and thinking the worst about my safety, so I just went straight into the nearest VicRoads office in a panic. My mind was in overdrive wondering whether Marty would be able to find out details about me. I was in panic mode, overthinking everything.

I also had to ring my bank, whose staff were very helpful. A lovely customer service person put my mind at rest. She made notes on my file that I was a former Optus customer and to flag any strange activity on my account. I also had to update my Medicare card—yet more life admin that I could do without. Later I discovered that VicRoads have a domestic violence phone number, so I called that explaining my situation. By early October I had a casefile with them and was finally starting to feel less stressed. Then Optus sent me an email, which began: 'Dear Dianne... It is with great disappointment I'm writing to let you know that Optus has been a victim of a cyberattack.' A bit late, Optus. The company's claim that they had released a statement to the media before informing customers as 'the quickest and most effective way to alert you' didn't give me much comfort. Around this time I also signed up for the class action with Slater & Gordon. I spoke to one of their lawyers and said I'd be happy to speak publicly about the stress this experience has caused. Marty Norman may have been punished for what he did to me, but the fallout was relentless.

FACEBOOK IS WONDERFUL for taking you back down memory lane. On 7 January 2023, a post came up from 2017. Marty had struck again on this day at the two wine bars and put up more of his offensive flyers. This date was also just days before the first anniversary of Cathie's death. Even though the post was now just a memory, it was a reminder that I still needed to be vigilant. Marty's two-year community corrections order was due to end on 10 January, taking away the last effective legal protection I had against him attacking me. While I still had an intervention order against him, he had shown in the past that it meant nothing to him. To say I was worried is an understatement.

But I still had a few days of freedom; freedom to create happy memories with my children. I was very aware at this time that I needed to do that, as the last seven years had been hell. Shania Twain toured Melbourne in late 2022, so I took Rhiannon to see her and we were both blown away by her performance. For Christmas, I gave all the kids a death-defying experience—a chance to ride the Firefly zipline that goes across the Yarra River. The Yarra, whose Indigenous name is 'Birrung', is a murky shade of brown and not a river you'd want to go swimming in, so I hoped we wouldn't fall off the zipline! When I told the organisers I'd recently had a hip replacement, they freaked out. The look on their faces was priceless.

Thankfully, 10 January came and went without incident. Other than the useless intervention order, Marty now had no limitations on him for the first time since being released from jail, but I tried to put thoughts like that out of my mind. The next day was Amity's birthday, so we had a reason to celebrate and forget about Marty.

The sixth anniversary of Cathie's death was on 15 January. It doesn't get any easier, but I spent the day with my friend Nicole. She's always fun, and she kept my mind busy. The next anniversary I had to face was that of Karen Chetcuti's passing, which come close on the heels of Cathie's sad date. This is always a hard time of year for me, but I went out with the girls for another gig. I'm glad I have amazing people in my life that keep me busy, otherwise I'd be home stressing and overthinking. PTSD is such a curse.

Meanwhile I kept busy creating awareness about stalking by appearing in the media. I was asked to speak at the State Library at a forum on stalking organised by former homicide detective Narelle Fraser. Afterwards she asked me to be on her podcast. We recorded on 13 March and I spoke for an hour and a half. I had a lot to say, so Narelle published the podcast in two parts. They were released in early April and titled 'Di McDonald and the Narcissist' as part of the 'Narelle Fraser Interviews' on Apple podcasts.

Around this time I also reached out to David Limbrick MP. When Tania Maxwell had issued amendments to the Victims of Crime Compensation Act, I heard David speak about his personal experience with stalking and thought he might be able to help with establishing a stalking awareness movement. He gave a powerful speech about his high school girlfriend, who was stalked and killed by the Frankston murderer. She was just seventeen years old, and the murderer's last victim. The experience scarred David for life, as trauma does.

David was more than happy to connect with me. I had a meeting with him and his staff, including his media adviser, Gavin. They wanted me to speak to the media about some proposed compulsory changes to regulations governing the health records of Victorians. The proposed change would allow anyone in the medical field to access a patient's medical records. It was to be compulsory, with no opt out option. Similar changes had already been made at the federal level, but in that instance patients could choose to opt out. I chose to opt out, because keeping my information private is one way I can protect myself from potential attacks from Marty. I'm sure that any victim of violence would do the same.

I agreed to speak on this issue, and on 23 February I fronted the media in the gardens of Parliament House. I said the proposed changes were against our human rights, and asked where was an individual's right to decide who has access to extremely private information. The media conference was on every news channel, but unfortunately this experience left me with a bad taste in my mouth...

The proposed changes to the Bill were tabled on 8 March, and David Limbrick gave an empowering speech to open the debate. I was extremely humbled by David's description of me as 'the bravest person he's ever met'. Unfortunately the Bill was passed, with one MP saying some not so nice things about 'a stalking victim'—by whom he clearly meant me. He claimed that a victim of stalking was being used to create a 'false equivalency' with human rights breaches. I was given a right of reply to these comments, and submitted a letter to be read out in Parliament in which I defended my comments and reiterated the dangers posed by the changes to the Bill. Among other things, I said:

> Will the Government guarantee our safety should our informa-
> tion be leaked? How are you going to help us?... The current
> Government needs to move with the times and move on from
> their dinosaur attitudes and realise how the technology world
> works before more lives are lost...

After this drama in Parliament, the *Herald Sun* newspaper contacted me for comments on what happened. Of course I was only too willing to give them my thoughts. My friends had started saying I was becoming a force to be reckoned with, which was nice to hear.

In June I attended the Brighton Lunch, which is a fundraiser for domestic violence. Rosie Batty and Lloyd and Sue Clarke—the parents of Hannah Clarke, who along with her three children was murdered by her husband in 2020—all spoke that day. It was a great afternoon—my friend Nicole came with me and we caught up with Tania Maxwell as well. I had to leave early as I had plans, but apparently Nicole and Tania ended up partying into the wee hours of the morning!

Narelle Fraser, who I'd done a podcast with, asked me to speak at another forum, which she called 'The Stalker' this time for a Crime Night to be held at a local venue in August. The night was a success, with over 300 people in attendance, and I was rapt to have (now former) detective Beck Norris there. Beck has become a close friend and attends most things I do. I felt at home on stage, and our presentation received a standing ovation. Afterwards people lined up to speak to me and to hear more about my story. Many of them asked if I was writing a book. Narelle decided to organise a second show.

Two weeks later I met up with Beck Norris again, this time to film a podcast with former FBI Agent Ray Carr and our old friend James R. Fitzgerald. Again, it had to be a two-part podcast as we had so much to discuss. Immediately afterwards I recorded a podcast with Vikki Petraitis, a well-known crime author and podcaster. The first episode of Jim and Ray's podcast, *Cold Red: A Stalker from Down Under*, dropped on 2 September, and people commented they were hooked and wanted more.

LEFT Sitting by the *Lost Petition* on the steps of Parliament House

RIGHT My surprise 60th birthday party, surrounded by friends and family

I hoped that I was getting the message out there; it was sorely needed. Australia was in the grip of a domestic violence epidemic. In 2022, when I recorded these podcasts, thirty-five women were killed in Australia by an intimate partner, and a total of fifty-six women were killed by a man. One of the most high-profile cases was that of Celeste Manno, whose death prompted the VLRC enquiry into stalking law reform. I had met Celeste's mother, Aggie di Mauro, in a parliamentary meeting in 2021 and we had been in touch ever since. Aggie was organising a vigil for Celeste on the steps of Parliament House to highlight how dangerous stalking is and that more needs to be done about awareness of it. The vigil was to take place on 18 October and I started promoting it in September, hoping to get as many people as possible to attend.

On the day of the vigil, the weather was cold but the rain stayed away. An artwork called the *Lost Petition* was displayed, which depicted the names of 1,084 murdered women. The women are listed by the year they were murdered. I found my childhood friend Karen Chetcuti's name and sat near it for the vigil. Parliament was still in session at the time and a few MPs came out to speak to people. The *Lost Petition* is an ongoing artwork, and since that night the names of many more women and children have been added.

I'd had a busy 2023, in November I had a personal milestone—I turned sixty—and my girls organised a surprise party for me. It was such a fabulous thing for them to do, and not easy. My Facebook settings are so tight they had trouble getting hold of any of my friends. They were a bit disappointed that they couldn't find more people to invite, but we had a wonderful evening nonetheless.

CHAPTER 11

SADA

IN THE YEARS since Marty Norman was jailed, I had become increasingly busy trying to do my bit to improve laws around stalking and its dangers and also about privacy in Victoria, spreading the word through podcasts, interviews and personal appearances. Mostly I had reacted to people reaching out to me, but I was also trying to be proactive.

I became aware that January is stalking awareness month in the USA. The colour used for the ribbon is yellow. As yellow is the colour of cowardice, I thought this very fitting. When I heard about this initiative, it occurred to me that Australia had nothing like it. Perhaps we should have. In February 2023 I decided to try to implement some sort of stalking awareness program in Australia. I emailed our Prime Minister and advised him that Joe Biden had been promoting it. I crossed my fingers and hoped I would hear something back from the PM. Meanwhile I also implemented a petition to make Stalking Awareness Month a reality and began to speak about it on the podcasts I was invited to appear on. My hope was that Australia could also have it in January.

In March I received a reply from the Prime Minister's office. They were very interested in what I had to say and asked me to organise a meeting with the Social Services Minister, Amanda Rishworth. I reached out to Amanda immediately. Of course, nothing moves quickly when it comes to government matters, but eventually Amanda's executive assistant referred me to her advisor, Kate Coleman, who reached out to set up a Teams meeting.

I was then referred to Victoria's peak body for domestic violence, and I talked to them about the need for some sort of pamphlet or booklet with guidelines on how to handle stalking. I thought this could be useful for both victims and police. Unfortunately, they really didn't understand what I was talking about. Even though I had sent them a prototype of an information booklet I had created, they kept saying there was already a lot of educational information available about 'domestic violence'. I replied by saying that stalking is not the same as domestic violence, that there are important differences and we need help and guidance tailored to stalking. Sadly this initiative came to a dead end. It is so hard to get people to understand stalking and why it is so dangerous.

I decided to reach out to David Limbrick to see if he could help me initiate a formal stalking awareness day or month in Australia. David's press officer, Gavin, contacted me and said he would like to start a foundation or something to make this happen. Knowing that stalking awareness month might actually happen had me on a high. Gavin also told me he had nominated me for a 'Local Heroes' award. So nice of him to do that.

After a lot of deliberation with Gavin, we finally announced Stalking Awareness Day Australia (SADA). We were going back and forth with names as we couldn't find something that hadn't already been registered as a

Beth, Gavin & me: the SADA team inside Parliament House

domain name for a website. Then finally, we have it: SADA is born, with the date fixed for 24 May as part of Domestic Violence Prevention Month. I had originally wanted 28 May to honour Cathie, as she was a 28 baby, but that date was taken by the LGBTQIA+ group. I then looked at 11 May, but 'Dolly's Dream' is around that time. This is to honour Dolly, who lost her life after being extensively bullied and cyberbullied. The 24th was available, and we all agreed on that date. It wasn't the full month of January, as I had hoped, but I was so happy to have something official locked in. I then started designing a logo; I was thinking a phoenix, which signifies a victim rising from the ashes to become a survivor. Then I tried out various colours before settling on black and gold.

I was back at Parliament House for a meeting with David and his staff on 2 February 2024, and used the opportunity to shoot a video for the SADA website while in the library. I wasn't prepared for it, but I think it came across okay. I filmed it with Gavin and one of David's staff members, Beth, who handles all his social media and was creating all the social pages for SADA. As staying off social media is one way I can protect myself, I can't do this myself. I couldn't believe all this was actually happening.

Later in February I headed to Sydney to film an episode of *Insight* for SBS, entitled 'Being Watched'. The filming was great and it gave me a chance to speak about SADA. While I was there I met Grant Killen, a former policeman, who has started a company to help victims of crime check for bugs and trackers. I asked if I could add his details to the SADA website. Grant was hoping to open offices all over Australia, and I offered to work for him if he opens a Victorian office. He agreed that there's no better qualification than lived experience!

On *Insight*, I also mentioned the safety watch the StandbyU Foundation had given me. The day after the episode aired in April, Chris from the foundation contacted me and thanked me for discussing the watch and how it works. He had been inundated with requests for a watch or, as the StandbyU Foundation call it, a safety shield. It was fantastic to hear I was reaching people with my story and helping them learn how to keep themselves safe.

Meanwhile I had also started ordering SADA merchandise in the form of t-shirts and tote bags. Narelle Fraser had organised a second Crime Night on 21 February, and I brought all my SADA merchandise with me. Beck Norris and Gavin were there, and I brought SADA merch for all of them and wore my SADA t-shirt on stage.

Gavin organised a press conference at Parliament House to launch Stalking Awareness Day Australia on 7 March. Again, I brought in t-shirts for everyone to wear. Vikki Petraitis, Narelle Fraser, Tania Maxwell and David Limbrick took turns to speak. The next day was International Women's Day, and that night Channel Nine formally announced Stalking Awareness Day Australia on their 6 pm news. My phone *exploded* with messages and calls.

SADA continued to gain momentum. I was asked to appear on TNT Radio with Chris Smith to talk about SADA and *Australian Story*. Three days before I was due to appear, the massacre at Bondi Junction Westfield took place, in which six people were killed and twelve injured. Live on air on 16 April, Chris asked me about the stabbings and if women should be allowed to carry pepper spray, which is currently illegal. I answered yes, as otherwise women are defenceless. With the growing numbers of women being murdered, something needs to be done. We were—and still are—in a domestic violence epidemic.

On 28 April, a 'National Rally Against Violence' was held in every state in Australia. In a speech, Prime Minister Anthony Albanese declared that Australia faced a 'national crisis' of violence against women, with one woman being killed every four days. I attended the Sunday rally with Gavin and both of us wore our SADA t-shirts. Aggie di Mauro and her family were there, and carried banners for Celeste that expressed their disappointment with the courts and the sentence given to Celeste's murderer.

The next day my sister, Michelle, got in touch and told me her employer, Bendigo Bank, was on board to highlight SADA. They have a 'casual for a cause' day, so staff will come to work out of uniform and in casual clothes, and put up posters to promote SADA. Michelle went one step further by putting a link in their newsletter so the bank staff could buy their own t-shirts. It was unbelievable, the support I was getting. I was so grateful.

Of course, if the Bendigo Bank was going to put up posters, they would need some! It was then I realised that I needed to have one designed. I contacted my dear friend Terry, who came up with a couple of amazing designs, one of which was terrifyingly spooky. I couldn't thank him enough. I sent both designs through to my sister who arranged to have them put up at all the Victorian Bendigo Bank branches.

I also had to organise a press conference for SADA, and had a meeting with David Limbrick and Gavin. Gavin asked if there was somewhere significant I would like to hold it other than Parliament House. I very quickly answered, 'the Winelarder.' Gavin wasn't so sure, but he eventually came around to this idea and started organising TV, newspapers and women's magazines to cover it.

My next phone call was to Christine from the Winelarder to ask permission to hold the press conference there. I was so pleased that she said yes. To promote the day, I also asked if I could put up 'posters and flyers' on the front doors. We both laughed—it was definitely a full circle moment.

Beth and I then start blanketing all social media sites with Terry's posters. My dear friend Kathy Kaplan AO, who started Impact, the organisation I volunteered at, put up a post for Stalking Awareness Day Australia. Bless her. And Crime Watch Victoria also came on board to promote SADA. It was generating a lot of buzz, but as 24 May approached, I was feeling nervous. What if no one from the press turned up? But I needn't have worried...

Several reporters and journalists were there. Channel 7 ran two reports, one for their 4 pm news hour and the other for the 6 pm news. I spoke on camera, as did Narelle Fraser, David Limbrick and Aggie Di Mauro. Also, NewsCorp were there and Lily McCaffrey, a reporter with NewsCorp, ran a great story in the print media realm. On their socials, Channel 7 ran with the photo of us putting up posters on the Winelarder's windows, reclaiming the venue that had been the scene of so many of Marty's sordid attacks.

Beck Norris, who was by now retired from the police force, still comes to all the events I do for stalking awareness. She arrived at the Winelarder for the SADA press conference with the biggest flower arrangement I'd ever seen. I was a bit overwhelmed, and she said to me, 'Don't read the card until later.' It was good advice, as I'd have been in a puddle of tears if I had. After the press conference and the lunch, when I was on my way home to do a radio interview, Beck messaged me and said, 'Do you know what you've accomplished?' That became clear when I learned that Victoria Police had recognised SADA. And that was when I finally broke down with happy tears.

This was VicPol's statement:

Today is Stalking Awareness Day Australia.

This is an important initiative to raise awareness about stalking, and how people can seek support.

A stalker can be an ex-partner, a family member, or a friend. It could also be someone less well known, like a colleague or someone who lives in the neighbourhood, or even a complete stranger.

There are four ways to identify stalking:

- **Fixated:** *Does the perpetrator find different ways to get the attention of the victim or try to become part of their life?*

- **Obsessive:** *Does the perpetrator always want to know where the victim is and what they are doing?*

- **Unwanted:** *Has the perpetrator been told to stop?*

- **Repeated:** *Does the perpetrator continue to contact the victim?*

Everyone deserves to feel safe.

If you feel unsafe and believe you are being stalked, we encourage you to speak to your local police.

In an emergency, please call Triple Zero (000).

It's done, and everyone knows about it and they're supporting SADA. I feel I can relax now; I've accomplished something great that was only a dream. I've pushed myself to get this done and I'm proud of myself and the legacy I am creating...

WELCOME TO THE WORLD
STALKING AWARENESS DAY AUSTRALIA
MAY YOU HELP SOMEONE IN NEED
TO KNOW THEY'RE NOT ALONE

EPILOGUE

TWO DAYS AFTER SADA launched, Aggie di Mauro had a rally at Parliament House to promote justice for her daughter Celeste. Of course I was there—there was still work to do. After the rally I had to go and film for that night's episode of *The Project*, whose producers had asked if I would appear on camera to discuss SADA. I enjoyed the filming—I would even say it was fun. I was more relaxed now that SADA had had its inaugural day, and I was equally happy with the report that aired that night.

Hume Shire Council also came on board to promote SADA. It was at their libraries that Marty created the offensive flyers he posted about me. I was asked to attend a meeting to advise them on how to do better and what to look out for. At the meeting they offered their regret and sadness that things were not done to stop Marty. They now have better policies in place to deal with such a situation. That was another full circle moment for me. They also asked me to take part in their sixteen days of activism as a guest speaker later in 2024. Of course, I accepted.

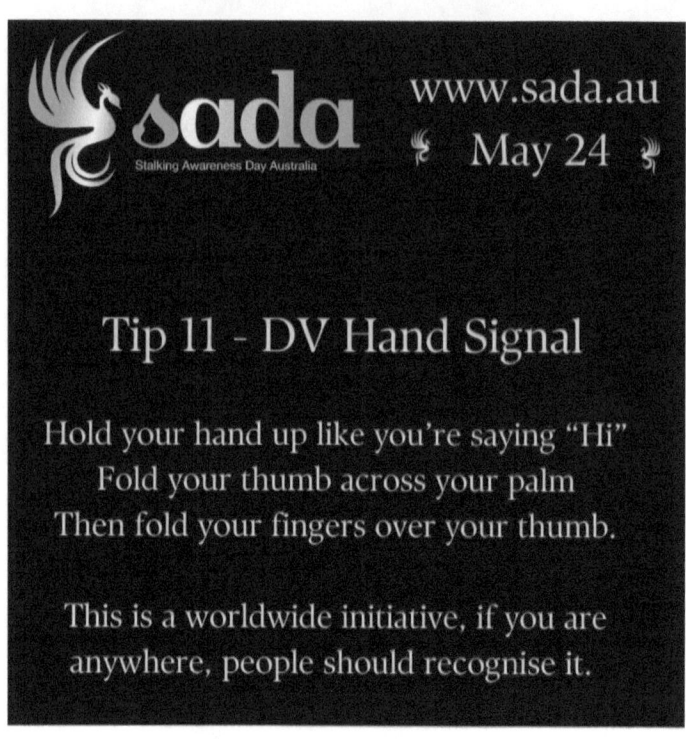

One of our social tiles with tips for victims

On 1 July 2024, I celebrated the introduction of coercive control laws in New South Wales. Legislation had been passed back in 2022 to make coercive control a crime, and the two years that had since passed were used to educate the police, the judiciary and the public. Offenders can receive up to seven years if convicted and, to keep victims safe, they won't receive bail. Finally a government was considering a victim's human rights. Well done, New South Wales. Let's hope Victoria gets on board with this as well.

In other good news, my neighbour contacted me asking if I would mind being interviewed by her daughter for her VCE piece, which is about stalking. I'm excited to have teenagers interested in the topic. I sent through links to both the *Australian Story* episodes, the website and some of the social tiles with tips for victims of violence that we've created. So glad the word about SADA is getting out there.

But we have a long way to go... The VLRC report on stalking law reform was submitted in 2022. That year, fifty-six women were killed by men in Australia; in 2023, sixty-four women were killed by men in Australia; in 2024, 101 women were killed by men in Australia. Men are also victims of domestic and gendered violence.

Stalking is not physical violence, but it is often a precursor to violence. In Australia, one in five women and one in fifteen men experience stalking.[2] At the time of writing, over two years since the VLRC report was tabled, sadly none of its forty-five recommendations have been implemented.

AT THE END of the second episode of *Australian Story;* 'To Catch a Stalker', the words 'Di McDonald is putting her house on the market and wants to change her name' appeared on the screen. I did neither of those things. I didn't sell my beautiful cottage in Craigieburn until January 2025, closing a chapter of my life. And I am still Di McDonald—advocate and activist.

---

2   https://www.abs.gov.au/media-centre/media-releases/1-7-australians-have-been-stalked

A FINAL WORD

IF YOU ARE feeling helpless, take a chance, think outside the box. It may just save you...

- If I hadn't joined a Facebook group called Protect Victoria and gone to a meeting, I wouldn't have met the Members of Parliament who helped me.

- If Cathie's friend Katie hadn't reached out to me when Cathie died, and invited me to her art class, I wouldn't have met Cheryl Hall from the ABC.

These two things changed my path. I had to push myself to go, but I'm forever grateful that I did.

RESOURCES

Stalking Awareness Day Australia:
www.sada.au
Read the SADA booklet here:
https://siliconwebsolutions.in/Sada/wp-content/
uploads/2024/02/Stalking-Awareness-Information-
Booklet.pdf

National Domestic, Family and Sexual Violence Counselling Service:
www.1800respect.org.au

State services for victims of crime:

- VIC Victims of Crime Helpline: 1800 819 817
- NSW Victims Access Line: 1800 633 063
- QLD Victim Assist: 1300 546 587
- SA Victims of Crime: 08 7322 7007
- WA Victim Support Service: 1800 818 988
- NT Victims of Crime: 1800 672 242
- ACT Victim Support: 1800 822 272
- TAS Victims of Crime Service: 1300 300 238

StandbyU Foundation (Chris Boyle): www.standbyu.org.au

Safety and security measures for victim-survivors (Grant Killen):

www.concentricconcepts.com.au

Information about stalking laws: https://privacy.org.au/resources/privacy-law/australia/

Information about cyberstalking:

https://www.esafety.gov.au/key-topics/staying-safe/cyberstalking

Media

Australian Story: 'To Catch a Stalker' (Parts 1 & 2 available on ABC iview and YouTube)

Podcasts

Best Case—Worst Case: 'Points of Ellipses' (released 7 July 2020)

Strictly Stalking: 'Killing Her Slowly' (released 23 February 2021)

Narelle Fraser Interviews: 'Di McDonald and the Narcissist' Part 1 (released 29 March 2023)

Narelle Fraser Interviews: 'Di McDonald and the Narcissist' Part 2 (released 5 April 2023)

Cold Red: 'Di McDonald's Story—A Stalker from Down Under' Part 1 (released 1 September 2023)

Cold Red: 'Di McDonald's Story—A Stalker from Down Under' Part 2 (released 8 September 2023)

Narelle Fraser Interviews: 'Di McDonald' (released 22 May 2024)

Life Matters: 'What to Do About Stalking' (released 31 October 2024, available on ABC Listen)

Motive & Method: 'He could attack at any time. The woman who was stalked' (released 4 December 2024)

Casefile Presents: 'Vikki Petratis, Beck Norris & Di McDonald' Part 1 (released 29 December 2024)

Casefile Presents: 'Vikki Petratis, Beck Norris & Di McDonald' Part 2 (released 5 January 2025)

THE FLYERS

THESE ARE the flyers that were posted at various venues and locations.

WINE Larder

INVATATION

Free Entry

Guys, drop in and enjoy viewing the sad, cheap antics of Dianne McDonald, as she flirts her way to seedy sexual satisfaction.

Obviously she has no morals, otherwise she would know that she has made a cheap name for herself, and a reputation to match.

This woman has set all records for the amount of different men she has been with in this bar.

The more wine, the more she flirts, and the more the legs open.

Wine larder

Address: 1/153 Martin St, Brighton VIC 3186

To the Manager:

Thank you for a most enjoyable night at your wine bar.

From my previous involvement with the Vice Squad and as a Private Investigator, my concern at your wine bar was the offensive, promiscuous , flirtatious behaviour of a certain Dianne McDonald, bordering on prostitution. Also the dress code of this woman has all the signs of a working class old tart.

My other concern is that this woman may be practicing out of your establishment.

Then again, it is only prostitution if charges are laid, otherwise it's just whoring.

In my opinion this over intoxicated woman has had more pricks than a second hand dart board, and her behaviour can only give your bar a bad name.

I'm happy to place this review online

A concerned patron .

How ironic , that Dianne McDonald , a woman that cheated on her husband, abandoned her children is nothing but gutter trash and the biggest slut in Victoria, wants to lead in a march for women and ending up at the BUFVALE Hotel.

This is laughable and an insult to genuine women that have morals.

Dianne McDonald is so ignorant that she doesn't realise that she has a huge reputation around town and within the music industry as a cheap whore.

Congratulations to you and your slut of a girlfriend for being recognised as some of the biggest whores in Melbourne.

Ignorance is NO excuse, but if you choose to dress like a whore, then you will be taken for a whore.

Ignorance is NO excuse, but if you constantly wish to flirt and act like a whore, then you will certainly be labelled a whore.

Ignorance is NO excuse, but when you openly make sexual statements and advances or gestures towards your girlfriend, then this is taken as uncomfortable, embarrassing and unacceptable.

Ignorance is NO excuse, but this type of conduct rather than parenting properly can only psychologically damage your children as to the proper, responsible and moral way to act.

Ignorance is NO excuse, but for you both not to realise that people do talk and laugh about you behind your backs is embarrassing, and for you both not to realise that you have gained a reputation as second rate whores, is astonishing.

Tweedle Dee and Tweedle Dum   ?

Cathie   *Dianne*

No   No   No

<u>Dumb and Dumber</u>   ?

Dianne   *Cathie*

No   No   No

Just **two** *pathetic old whores*

Who have gained an embarrassing reputation in the community as second rate, trailer trash sluts !!!!

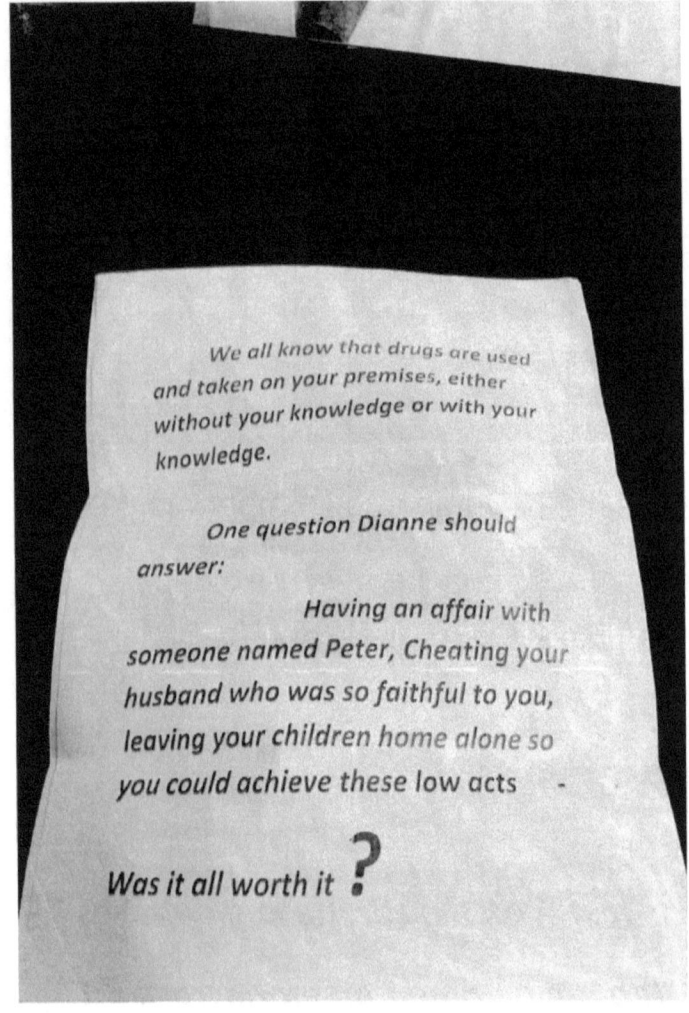

We all know that drugs are used and taken on your premises, either without your knowledge or with your knowledge.

One question Dianne should answer:

Having an affair with someone named Peter, Cheating your husband who was so faithful to you, leaving your children home alone so you could achieve these low acts   -

Was it all worth it **?**

WoooHoooooo,

Welcome back Dee Dee's dirty little
whore house, with cheap brothel photo's to boot.

You have done an excellent job at disgracing,
embarrassing and humiliating the Woodbridge name.

JOKE

The truth is,

Dianne did neglect her children and cheated on her husband.

She is a Total disgrace
as a so called mother

THE Brighton, cheating Bimbo's

Oh how the truth must hurt, but one day they
will have to accept the truth rather than pretending
nothing has ever happened and going out dressed like
cheap tramps.

Failed as wife, failed as a mother and would more
than likely be the embarrassment of the family –
does this ring any bells.

Is this the way venues in Brighton get customers
in by having these whores parading around like
second rate hookers ?

How embarrassing

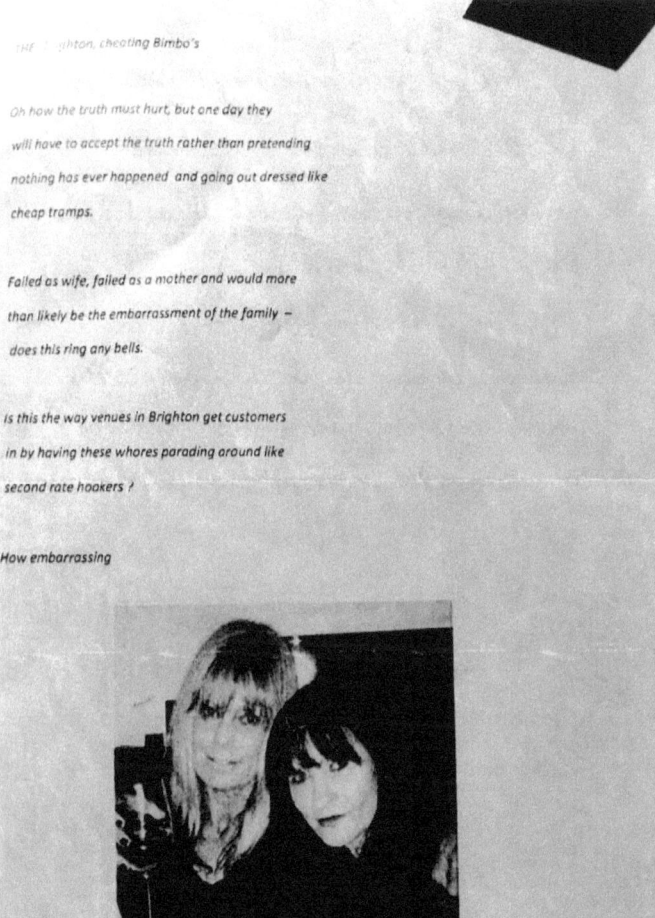

We all pray that this troll

Dianne will for once write

something on the internet that has

honesty in it, like:

Her leaving her children

home alone at night, unsupervised,

with no safety, just so she could go

and cheat on their father.

Amen

And that she has had more

pricks in her than a second hand

dart board.

Allelujah   Amen

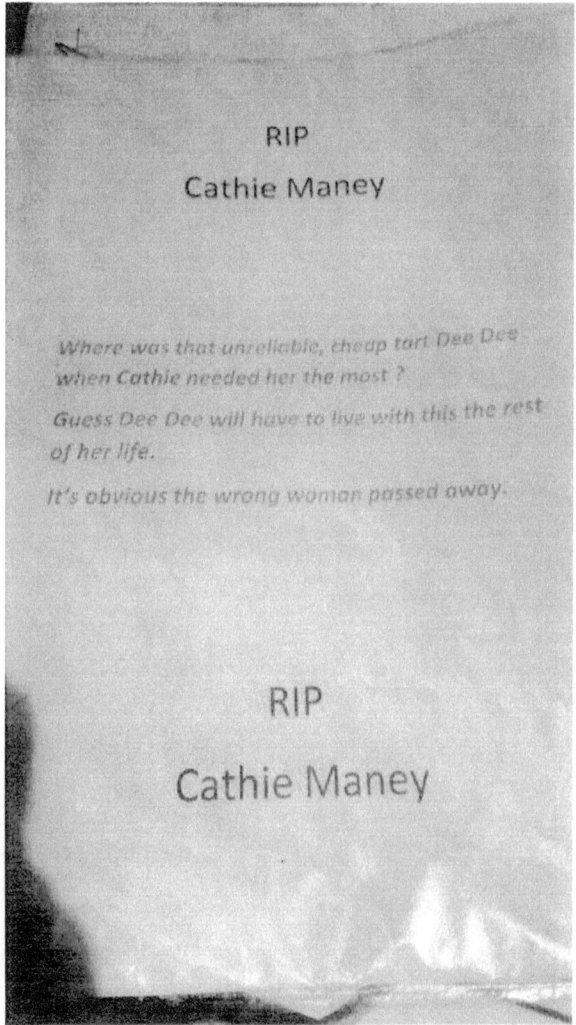

RIP

Cathie Maney

Where was that unreliable, cheap tart Dee Dee
when Cathie needed her the most ?

Guess Dee Dee will have to live with this the rest
of her life.

It's obvious the wrong woman passed away.

RIP

Cathie Maney

RIP
21.1.17

For you Dee Dee,
You were such a bad influence to Cathie and
used her for your own cheaps thrills.

"So many took advantage

So many manipulated behind the
scenes

They didn't realize how fragile
you were

Or perhaps they did

And if so, they have blood
on their hands"

R.I.P

Cathie Maney

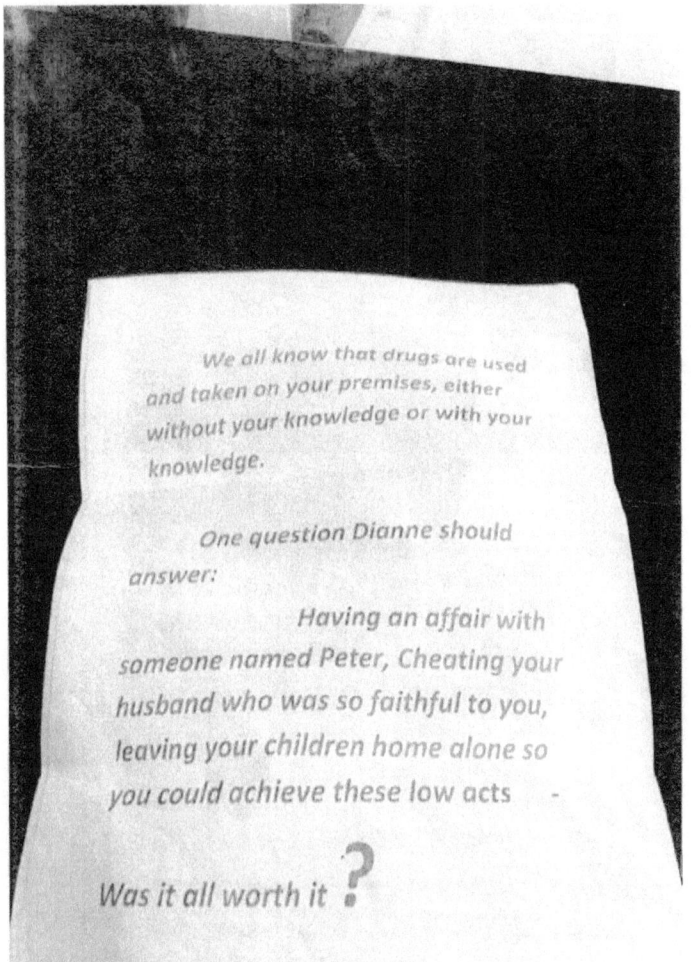

We all know that drugs are used and taken on your premises, either without your knowledge or with your knowledge.

One question Dianne should answer:

Having an affair with someone named Peter, Cheating your husband who was so faithful to you, leaving your children home alone so you could achieve these low acts   -

Was it all worth it ?

Oh NO, just when we were all comfortable and enjoying going out, that Brighton Bitch, Cathie killer, Dianne McDonald comes back from O'seas and continues to be the cheap slut that she is.

Now Dianne is wishing that she was back there.

So we all say, the sooner the better.

Allelujah, we are taking donations to see that this happens ASAP.

Considering that the only thing that Dianne can show her children, is the abusive cheating person she is, which they all would have witnessed by her crude actions to their father.

Yes, Dianne McDonald was unfaithful to her husband, and is trailer trash.

So please, back you go.

We don't want your type here.

HOW BIZARRE,

NORMALLY DIANNE IS STANDING NEXT TO A STREET POLE ON THE STREETS IN STKILDA

*SECOND RATE **HOOKER***

BLESSED ?

BLESSED AT BEING A FILTHY,
SMELLY, CHEAP, UNFAITHFUL,
CHEATING SLUT

After contributing to Cathie's demise, why didn't Dianne just drive over the cliff like Thelma and Louise, and finally make everyone happy.

Blessed

BLESSED ?

Agree a Cunt

BLESSED AT BEING A FILTHY, SMELLY, CHEAP, UNFAITHFUL, CHEATING SLUT

So naïve of you not to recognise the undercover, illegal, seedy little brothels set up locally, with the head act Dianne McDonald who has more pricks in her than a second hand dart board.

How morally confused you must be to ignore the well orchestrated acts, bordering on soliciting by Dianne McDonald.

We all know, as does the local community, that Dianne controlled, used and abused Cathie, and that Dianne now has and always will have, "Blood On Her Hands".

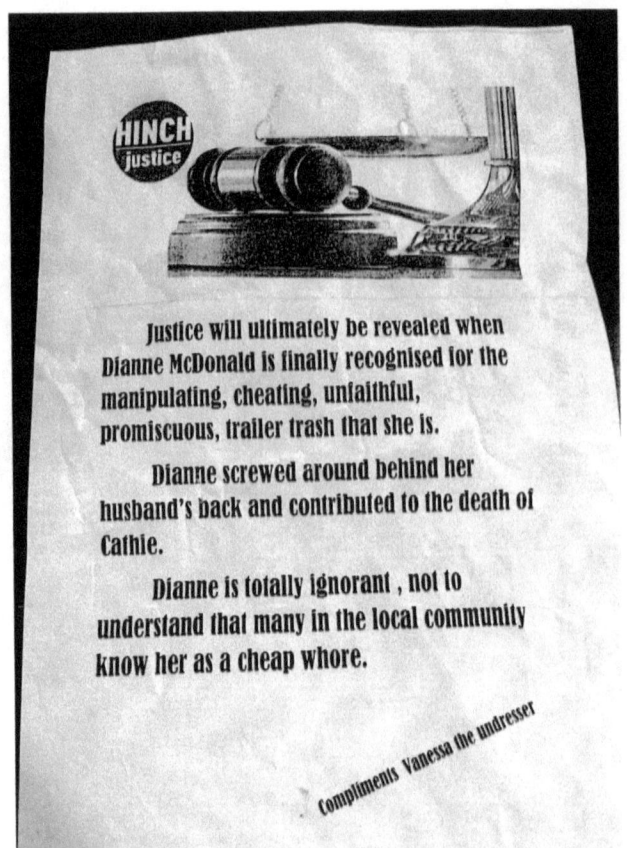

Justice will ultimately be revealed when Dianne McDonald is finally recognised for the manipulating, cheating, unfaithful, promiscuous, trailer trash that she is.

Dianne screwed around behind her husband's back and contributed to the death of Cathie.

Dianne is totally ignorant , not to understand that many in the local community know her as a cheap whore.

Compliments Vanessa the undresser

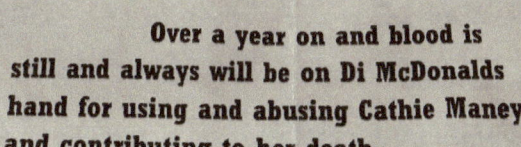

Over a year on and blood is still and always will be on Di McDonalds hand for using and abusing Cathie Maney and contributing to her death.

Lets all pray and hope that if Di McDonald has any children, that they haven't been damaged by their mother cheating on their father, and that they haven't been influenced by their mother's filthy, promiscuous ways.

Just a dirty cheap whore, as all the community knows.

We all pray that this troll

Dianne will for once write

something on the internet that has

honesty in it, like:

Her leaving her children

home alone at night, unsupervised,

with no safety, just so she could go

and cheat on their father.

Amen

And that she has had more

pricks in her than a second hand

dart board.   Cunt

Allelujah   Amen

America has a Trump, we have a TRAMP.

Trying to earn more money again next to a street pole.

Do the Australian Taxation Department know about this ugly piece of TRASH.

APPENDIX 2

LINGUISTIC ANALYSIS REPORT

⒥ Ⓡ Ⓕ
James R. Fitzgerald Associates, LLC
615 Route 9 South #803
Cape May Court House, NJ 08210

February 7, 2019

Victoria Police Department

15 Dimboola Road, Broadmeadows

Victoria, Australia

Attn: Rebecca Norris, Detective Senior Constable

   ND4 Family Violence Unit

Re: JRFA Case No. 19-001

   Dianne McDonald - Harassing Anonymous
Letter Matter

FORENSIC LINGUISTIC/AUTHORIAL ATTRIBUTION ANALYSIS REPORT

INTRODUCTION

This forensic linguistic/authorial attribution analysis report was prepared by James R. Fitzgerald of James R. Fitzgerald Associates, LLC (JRFA). This assessment and analysis are based upon a review of 20 anonymous Questioned (Q) Communications received by or referencing Ms. Dianne McDonald and their comparison to seven Known (K) Communications authored by Mr. _____ _____.

As a result of a detailed forensic linguistic analysis, it is opined by JRFA that the overall writing style of ____ _____ as reflected in his seven Known Communications is <u>Consistent, to the degree of Exceptionally Distinctive*</u>, to the writing style found in the 20 anonymous Q Communications received by or referencing Dianne McDonald.

This analysis was undertaken to determine a linguistic linkage, if any, of the various Q Communications to the various K Communications of Mr. _____. The communications in this analysis were received by JRFA in electronic format from Detective Senior Constable Rebecca Norris.

The above and subsequent observations, opinions, and conclusions are the result of knowledge gained by investigative and analytical experience, specialized training and formal academic courses (to include a master's degree in Human Organizational Science and a master's degree in Linguistics), ongoing consultation with recognized experts in the field of forensic linguistics, and ongoing review of the relevant literature relating to this type of analysis. Mr. Fitzgerald has qualified numerous times as an expert in U.S. criminal and civil courts, at both the state and federal level, and has provided relevant testimony as such in the disciplines of text analysis and/or forensic linguistics.

In any text analysis of one or a collection of communications, whether spoken or written, it should be noted that every individual's speech and writing style is shaped by physiological and psychological factors including, but not limited to, gender, age, race, ethnicity, intelligence, geographic region, education, profession, and emotional development. Personal traits such as confidence, shyness, anger, resentment, emotionality, frustrated desire, and the like are manifest in a person's language no less than in his or her behavior. Moreover, every user of language has characteristic mannerisms with respect to orthography (spelling), punctuation, grammar, semantic usages, syntactical usages, and myriad stylistic choices. These all form what linguists refer to as a person's *idiolect*. The linguistic habits of one individual can possibly be found elsewhere in the writing or speech or another person or persons. Individuals within the same family, cultural group, profession, and/or geographic region may share many linguistic habits. However, it should be noted, unless quoting someone exactly word-for-word (including punctuation and formatting in written communications), no two individuals use words, or strings of words, precisely the same way whether speaking them or writing them.

This analysis is just one component of this case and should not be considered a substitute for a thorough, well-planned investigation, prosecution, defense, or civil litigation, nor should it necessarily be considered all-inclusive in its scope.

CASE SUMMARY

Other than JRFA being generally aware that numerous anonymous, harassing communications were received by and/or directly reference Dianne McDonald, with a possible suspect being a former significant other named _____ _____, the specifics and details of this matter which potentially link one or more of the assessed communications to one or more authors are unknown. To date, that information was neither provided by Det. Norris, the Victoria PD, nor requested or separately researched by JRFA.

THE COMMUNICATIONS

Questioned Communications

The Questioned (Q) Communications analyzed in this matter are as follows:

(Note: While there are 20 separate Q Communications listed below, only 17 of them are original. Three of them are duplicates of documents already received by Ms. McDonald at a previous time. The duplicate documents will be noted below.)

Q1 – computer generated, one-page document on standard-sized white stock paper, undated, unsigned, the body of which begins "Guys, drop in and...."

Q2 – computer generated, one-page document on standard-sized white stock paper, undated, unsigned, beginning "FREE BLOW..."

Q3 – computer generated, one-page document on standard-sized white stock paper, undated, unsigned, with photo, beginning "How ironic..."

Q4 – computer generated, one-page document on standard-sized white stock paper, undated, unsigned, beginning "Congratulations to you…"

Q5 – computer generated, one-page document on standard-sized white stock paper, undated, unsigned, beginning "Tweedle Dee and…"

Q6 – computer generated, one-page document on standard-sized white stock paper, undated, unsigned, beginning "RIP Cathie Maney."

Q7 – computer generated, one-page document on standard-sized white stock paper, undated, unsigned, beginning "For you Dee Dee."

Q8 – computer generated, four-page document on standard-sized white stock paper, undated, unsigned, with photo, beginning "After contributing…" It ends with "…a so called mother."

Q9 – computer generated, one-page document on standard-sized white stock paper, undated, unsigned, with photo, beginning "Justice will ultimately…"

Q10 – computer generated, one-page document on standard-sized stock paper, undated, unsigned, beginning "Over a year on…"

Q11 – duplicate of Q10 but utilizing a different font.

Q12 – duplicate of Q9.

Q13 – computer generated, one-page document on standard-sized white stock paper, undated, unsigned, the body of which begins "Thank you for a…"

Q14 – computer generated, one-page document on standard-sized white stock paper, undated, unsigned, with photo, the body of which begins "Blessed at being…"

Q15 – computer generated, one-page document on standard-sized white stock paper, undated, unsigned, beginning "We all pray…" Near the bottom of the document is the handwritten word "Cunt."

Q16 – duplicate of Q14.

Q17 – computer generated, one-page document on standard-sized white stock paper, undated, unsigned, with photo, beginning "WoooHoooooo…"

Q18 – computer generated, one-page document on standard-sized white stock paper, undated, unsigned, with photo, beginning "THE Brighton, cheating Bimbo's…"

Q19 – computer generated, two-page document on standard sized white stock paper, undated, unsigned, with photo, beginning "HOW BIZZARE..."

Q20 – computer generated, one-page document on standard sized white stock paper, undated, unsigned, with photo, beginning "America has a Trump..."

Known Communications

K1 – computer generated, three-page document on standard-sized white stock paper, undated, unsigned, the body of which begins "I am totally remorseful..."

K2 – computer generated, two-page document on standard-sized white stock paper, undated, unsigned, the body of which begins "I've had time to reflect..."

K3 – computer generated, one-page document on standard-sized white stock paper, undated, signed "_____," the body of which begins "When I gave you the..."

K4 – computer generated, five-page document on standard-sized white stock paper, undated, signed "_____ _____," the body of which begins "On the 14th of June..."

K5 – greeting card, undated, unsigned, cover of which reads "My partner, my love, my friend." Additional personalized handwriting is found inside card.

K6 – greeting card, undated, signed "_____," cover of which reads "Delightful you." Additional personalized handwriting is found inside card.

K7 – computer generated, three-page document on standard-sized white stock paper, undated, unsigned, the body of which begins "Please accept my sincere..."

AUTHORIAL ATTRIBUTION ANALYSIS

It should be noted that any text analysis for purposes of authorial attribution, and any subsequent linkage rendered as a result thereof, is only as extensive as the amount of spoken and/or written language involved. The more text available to review and compare, and/or the more distinctive, uncommon, and idiosyncratic linguistic features identified therein, the stronger the resulting rendered opinion as to authorship will be. Given the presence of a sufficient text sample and ample linguistic/stylistic evidence, an opinion of "Consistent" or "Not Consistent" may be rendered as to the fact that one individual, named or unnamed, is or is not linguistically associated with one or more questioned articles of text. Fewer text samples, and/or a lack of significant linguistic/stylistic evidence found therein, may result in an opinion of "No Decision" being rendered.

In this matter, within the 20 anonymous Qs and the seven Ks of Mr. _____, there is sufficient linguistic/stylistic evidence to render a tenable opinion as to common authorship features between them.

Initial Analysis

The first phase of this analysis was to compare the 20 Q Communications among themselves to determine if they were authored by one and the same person.

It is opined by JRFA that each of the 20 Qs was, in fact, authored by one and the same person.

The above opinion is based upon:

- The content of each Q document includes denigrating and insult-laden language about Dianne McDonald, much of it sexually oriented.
- They are each anonymous.
- Some include personal information ostensibly known only by a limited number of people.
- Some include photos purported to be that of Dianne McDonald.
- Virtually all paragraphs are indented.
- Virtually each paragraph consists of only one sentence.
- There is occasional extra spacing preceding certain marks of punctuation.
- There is occasional non-standard upper-case word-initial lettering.

- Postal transmittal envelopes for Q9, Q10, Q11, Q12, Q19, and Q20 were provided to JRFA for analysis. It is noted that each envelope has the identical postage stamp affixed to them. It is further noted that the address on each envelope is formatted in an unusual downward-then-inward/left-to-right indentation style.

Not each of the above indicators is necessarily found in every Q document. However, the totality of their combined presence spread throughout the 20 Qs is nonetheless very strongly suggestive of one author and one author only for all of them.

Secondary Analysis

The second phase of this analysis was to compare the 20 anonymous Q Communications to the seven K Communications of _____ _____. In doing so, each Q and K was carefully reviewed and assessed during this authorial attribution process. In the analysis, numerous lexical as well as other linguistic and stylistic parameters were used to assess each separate communication. Specific word usage, sentence structure, spelling, formatting, punctuation, as well as other standard and non-standard features, to one degree or another all contribute to the process of authorial attribution analysis. Each parameter can be as important as the other in this type of comparison and analysis, depending on its usage and the level of uncommonness and idiosyncratic nature in the examined communications.

It should be noted that there are several idiosyncratic features found in the 20 Qs and in the seven Ks of Mr. _____ which are virtually identical. These types of findings contribute greatly to any final opinion regarding potential common authorship. In addition, in this set of Q and K Communications there were, in fact, other noteworthy linguistic trends and patterns which were found in common among them. Measured qualitatively and quantitatively, these findings contribute greatly to the final opinion as to the potential of common authorship between the anonymous Q Communications and the K Communications of Mr. _____.

Linguistic/Stylistics Findings

A comparison of the writing style of the author of the 20 anonymous Q Communications and the writing style found in the seven K Communications of _____ _____ is below. This section will be divided into the following categories: General Observations, Formatting, Spelling, and Punctuation.

    A.   General Observations

- The author of the anonymous Qs and the author of the Ks, Mr. _____, both write the English language at a level approximating that of "above-average." The sentence structure, lexical choices, punctuation, and overall readability of each of the Qs and Ks reflects that of a person who is comfortable utilizing written English at a level beyond that of the casual writer. However, the Q and K documents both include uncommon and non-standard features (mistakes) within them. These will be examined in detail in subsequent categories in this report.

- The author of the Q Communications seems to have possessed at the time the documents were composed an advanced level of information and/or knowledge regarding Ms. McDonald involving at least some aspects of her personal life. Among other ostensibly accurate "facts" relating to Ms. McDonald, the author cites:

  - She frequents certain bars, i.e., Winelarder, and Elwood Food and Wine Bar;
  - A phone number potentially linked to her;
  - She may be somehow involved and/or interested in a "march for women" which ends at the Burvale Hotel;
  - She has a deceased friend named Cathie Maney;
  - She knows of a man named Peter;
  - She is/was married;
  - She may have been involved in an adulterous affair;
  - She is a mother.

If the above information was fully or even partially accurate at the time Ms. McDonald was in receipt of the various Q Communications, this is highly suggestive of the fact that the author at some point in the past had direct access to her in one capacity or another.

- Based on the consistent tone and the tenor of the content of the Q documents themselves, and the overall negativity therein as pertaining to Ms. McDonald, it is highly likely that the author feels he was wronged, slighted, and/or rejected by her in some form or manner. These feelings may be based in reality, or they may be based in perception. However, whether the former or the latter, it was enough in the mind of this author to commence and then continue an ongoing anonymous, harassing letter writing campaign for an extended period of time. In doing so, he was victimizing the real or perceived person deemed responsible for his alleged mistreatment - that being, Dianne McDonald.

B.   Formatting

- In the vast majority of the Q Communications, the author chooses to indent the first line of each paragraph. The exceptions to this feature are noted in Q6, in which there is a total of three paragraphs with no indentation; Q13, in which there is a total of six paragraphs with four not indented; Q18, in which there is a total of five paragraphs with no indentation; Q19, in which there is a total of nine paragraphs with four not indented; Q20, in which there is a total of three paragraphs with two not indented.
(Q2 is center aligned, thus indenting is not a factor. It is also not a factor in the two handwritten greeting cards.)

  There are 71 separate paragraphs in the relevant Q docs. 53 of these paragraphs are indented. Thus, 74.6% of the Q paragraphs are indented.

In the vast majority of the K Communications of Mr. _____, he chooses to indent   the first line of each paragraph. They are as follows:

- K1 – 19 paragraphs, 18 are indented
- K2 – 14 paragraphs, one is indented
- K3 – 5 paragraphs, 5 are indented
- K4 – 31 paragraphs, 29 are indented
- K7 – 33 paragraphs, 33 are indented

There are 102 paragraphs in the relevant K docs of Mr. _____. 86 of them are indented. Thus, 84.3% of the K paragraphs are indented.

The author of both the anonymous Qs and the Ks similarly chooses to indent the first line in the majority of the separate paragraphs within the two sets of documents. Interestingly, he seemingly utilizes a different number of spaces from one paragraph to another in many instances when choosing to indent. It is also noteworthy that the author does not indent every paragraph in those same documents. Among these non-indented paragraphs there is no readily observable pattern to them within the same document or even when compared to other Qs and Ks.

The choice to employ indentation within one's narrative writing style is not necessarily uncommon. What is uncommon is to find the aforementioned similar indenting inconsistencies within two otherwise very similar sets of documents (the Qs and the Ks), and at a relatively similar percentage rate (74.6% v 84.3%).

This feature contributes to the potential of common authorship between the two sets of documents.

- In the vast majority of the Q Communications, the author chooses to write each paragraph comprised of just one sentence. The only exception to this is noted in Q13 in which a paragraph is comprised of two sentences.

There are 71 separate paragraphs within the 17 relevant Qs and 70 of them contain only one sentence. Thus, 98.5% of the Q paragraphs contain only one sentence.

In the vast majority of the K Communications of Mr. _____, he chooses to write paragraphs comprised of just one sentence. They are as follows:

- K1 - 19 paragraphs, 16 are one sentence paragraphs
- K2 - 14 paragraphs, 11 are one sentence paragraphs
- K3 - 5 paragraphs, 5 are one sentence paragraphs
- K4 - 31 paragraphs, 27 are one sentence paragraphs
- K7 - 33 paragraphs, 29 are one sentence paragraphs

There are 102 paragraphs in the relevant Ks of Mr. _____. 88 of them are one sentence paragraphs. Thus, 86.2% of the K paragraphs are one sentence paragraphs. (The remaining 14 paragraphs are comprised of mostly two sentences, with only several being three sentences.)

Outside of formal journalistic-oriented publications, the choice to utilize repeated and frequent one sentence paragraphs within an individual's narrative writing style is relatively uncommon. What is additionally uncommon is to have this similar one sentence per paragraph consistency within two otherwise very similar sets of documents, and at a relatively similar percentage rate (98.5% v 86.2%).

This feature contributes to the potential of common authorship between the two sets of documents.

C.   Spelling

- Through either ignorance or carelessness, the author of the anonymous Q Communications chooses to utilize upper-case word-initial lettering in a non-standard fashion. Examples include (underlining added below for illustrative purposes):

  - Q5 – "Just two pathetic old whores <u>W</u>ho have gained an…"
  - Q8 – "Having an affair with someone named Peter, <u>C</u>heating your husband…"
  - Q8 – "She is a <u>T</u>otal disgrace as a so called mother."

  Through either ignorance or carelessness, the author of the K Communications, Mr. _____, chooses to utilize upper-case word-initial lettering in a non-standard fashion. Examples include (underlining added below for illustrative purposes):

- K2 – "You were an inspiration, an <u>A</u>ngel and such a beautiful woman…"
- K2 - "You said you had an awesome Melbourne Cup Day, <u>B</u>irthday and Christmas."
- K4 – "They advised me to go to the <u>P</u>olice about this."
- K4 – "I was attempting to ask the <u>P</u>olice that I wished to…"
- K4 - "The <u>P</u>olice advised me to go to…"
- K4 - "I felt the <u>P</u>olice should be made aware…"
- K4 – "…advised me to go to <u>C</u>ourt and fill in…"
- K4 – "I refute these FALSE allegations and <u>C</u>harges."
- K7 – "…would like to address this with my <u>C</u>ounsellor, to enable me to…"
- K7 – "I attempted to make your <u>B</u>irthday special."
- K7 – "I visited your Mum in <u>H</u>ospital."
- K7 – "I picked up your Mum from <u>H</u>ospital."

This feature contributes to the potential of common authorship between the two sets of documents.

- Apparently for purposes of emphasis, the author of the anonymous Q Communications chooses to occasionally utilize all upper-case lettering in a single mid-sentence word ("NO") to express negation. Examples include:

  - Q4 – "Ignorance is NO excuse…"
    (This is written five times to begin five separate paragraphs.)
  - Q19 – "Oh NO, just when we…"

Apparently for purposes of emphasis, the author of the K Communications, Mr. _____, chooses to occasionally utilize all upper-case lettering in a single mid-sentence word ("NO") to express negation. Examples include:

- K4 – "Obviously _____ had NO idea that her mother…"
- K4 – "At NO time did I interact…"
- K4 – "At NO time did I ever speak…"
- K4 – "…that at NO time did I ever…"

This feature contributes to the potential of common authorship between the two sets of documents.

- Through either ignorance or carelessness, the author of the anonymous Q Communications occasionally denotes pluralization and possessiveness and contractions in non-standard form. Examples include (italics and underlining added below for illustrative purposes):

  - Q10 – "…and always will be on Di McDonalds hand for using and abusing..." (It should read, "...Di McDonald_'s_ hand_s_... ")
  - Q10 – "Lets all pray and hope…" (It should read, "Let_'s all pray... ")

- Q17 – "…with cheap brothel photo_'s to boot."
  (It should read, "…*brothel photos to boot*."
- Q18 – "THE Brighton, cheating Bimbo_'s."
  (It should read, "…*cheating Bimbos*."

Through either ignorance or carelessness, the author of the K Communications, Mr. _____, occasionally denotes pluralization and possessiveness in non-standard form. Examples include (italics and underlining added below for illustrative purposes):

- K2 – "…have BBQ's and go away…"
  (It should read, "…*have BBQs and go away*…"
- K4 – "Diane McDonalds ex-husband."
  (It should read, "*Diane McDonald_'s ex-husband*.")
- K4 – "…around at her boy friends place."
  (It should read, "*…around at her boy friend_'s place*.")
- K4 – "…had left the mothers home…"

(It should read, "…*had left the mother's home*…")

- K4 – "…and went straight to Connors mens clothing store…"
  (It should read, "…*and went straight to Connor men's clothing store*…")
- K4 – "…due to Diane McDonalds (the mother) outburst…"
  (It should read, "…*due to Diane McDonald's (the mother's) outburst*…")
- K7 - "I am in shock, devastated and my hearts broken into pieces…"
  (It should read, "…*and my heart's broken into*…")

This feature contributes to the potential of common authorship between the two sets of documents.

D.   Punctuation

- For purposes seemingly related to emphasis, the author of the anonymous Q Communications chooses on one occasion to include an entirely boldened sentence mid-page in one of his letters to Ms. McDonald. It is:

Q3 – **"This is laughable and an insult to genuine women that have morals."**

For purposes seemingly related to emphasis, the author of the K Communications, Mr. _____, chooses on several occasions in one document to include entirely boldened sentences mid-page and beyond in one of his letters referencing Ms. McDonald. They are:

K4 – **"I strongly believe that my words were not fully heard whilst my head was turning** back to address the Police Officer or my words have been taken out of context."

K4 – "I have gotten on with my life, and I don't want anything to do with Dianne McDonald again."

K4 – "I refute the FALSE allegations and Charges."

This feature contributes to the potential of common authorship between the two sets of documents.

- Through either ignorance or carelessness, the author of the anonymous Q Communications on the one occasion in which he utilizes a mid-sentence dash ("- ") places extra spaces before and after it.

Q8 – "…these low acts   -
        Was it all worth it ?"
Q18 – "…of the family -
        does this ring any bells."

Through either ignorance or carelessness, the author of the K Communications, Mr. _____, on the several occasions in which he utilizes a mid-sentence dash, places extra spaces before and after it. Examples include:

K4 – "…and will never return   -   And that their son…"
K7 – "…by attending counselling   -   I never want to…"

This feature contributes to the potential of common authorship between the two sets of documents.

CONCLUSION

JRFA undertook a comprehensive authorial attribution analysis of the 20 anonymous Q Communications and the seven K Communications of ____ _____. This was undertaken to determine authorship commonalities, if any, between the two sets of communications.

In JRFA's analysis, the uncommonness and idiosyncratic nature of various features, to include the first line indenting frequency in both set of documents, the single sentence frequency in both set of documents, the non-standard possessive and pluralization instances in both sets of documents, along with the other noted repeated features found within the 20 documents, as well as the highly personal topical and thematic content of the Qs as they relate to Dianne McDonald, each serve to link _____ _____ to the Qs. As such, it is the opinion of JRFA that the writing style found within the Qs, when compared to the writing style of Mr. _____ in his seven Ks, is **CONSISTENT** to the degree of **Exceptionally Distinctive.***

There are naturally differences in some of the linguistic, lexical, and stylistic features within and between the Q Communications and the K Communications of Mr. _____. This is not unusual as language presents any writer/speaker with many and varied linguistic, lexical, and stylistic options from which to choose. However, the so-noted language commonalities between these two sets of Q and K writings, when taken in totality, firmly establishes the linkage between them and the fact that one author, _____ _____, is responsible for writing the Q Communications.

If there are any questions regarding this report, please feel free to contact James R. Fitzgerald at jfitzjourney@gmail.com.

The opinions and findings in this report assume that the information originally set forth to JRFA is reliable and valid. This analysis, and any subsequent opinions and conclusions, could be modified or changed should the investigation in this matter prove to invalidate the original information or documents upon which this analysis was based, or should the investigation provide new information or new documents related to the captioned matter.

This 13-page report is respectfully submitted to the Victoria Police Department, Victoria, Australia, on February 7, 2019.

James R. Fitzgerald

James R. Fitzgerald Associates, LLC

---

*Consistent Outcome – Distinctiveness Scale (in descending order):

5 Exceptionally Distinctive – There is only the remotest of possibilities that this combination of features is shared by other speakers/writers;

4 Highly Distinctive – There is very little possibility that this combination of features is shared by other speakers/writers;

3 Distinctive – There is a slight possibility that this combination of features is shared by other speakers/writers;

2 Moderately Distinctive – There is a possibility that this combination of features is shared by other speakers/writers;

1 Not Distinctive – There is a strong possibility that this combination of features is shared by other speakers/writers.

VICTIM IMPACT STATEMENT

THIS IS MY victim impact statement in full. The 'x's are the redacted portions that I was not allowed to read in court.

Your Honour, I stand before you today as one tin soldier who has lost her Xanadu but from this moment on will continue to pursue a new life, a vastly different life from what I knew for fifty-one years. My life now is fraught with insecurities, hyper-vigilance and fear. A fear of my safety, my children's, my mother's xxx xxxxxxxxxx xxx xxxx xxxxxxxxxxx xxxx xxx xx xxxx xxxxxx xxxxxx, xx xxx xxx xxxxxx xx xxx xxxx xxxx xxx xxxxxxxxx xx xx.

Since 2015 I have been dealing with a stalker, a stalker who has terrorised me regularly without any rhyme or reason. One way of terrorising me would be to post up disgusting flyers on two venue windows in Brighton and Elwood to offer my sexual services to strange men, xxxxxxxx xxxx xx xxxx xx xx xxxxx. xxxxxxx xx xxxx, to use my name, Cathie's name, photographs of us, Cathie's phone number, as I had changed my phone and number. The lies about me cheating on my husband, abandoning my children and the worst that I killed my best friend, Cathie. These flyers were put up in public places to generate maximum impact, but with one of the worst flyers, he lined the streets of Blackburn South through to Burwood when I was part of a public fundraising event to help the children of a lifelong friend who had been murdered. With this event there was maximum coverage from the media with Derryn Hinch being a part of the fundraiser and an article in the Herald Sun *and an interview on* A Current Affair. *Marty Norman used the photo of me out of the* Herald Sun *story. His plan failed as he lined the wrong side of the street with the media and Derryn walking on the side where the flyers weren't put up. Was he just trying to publicly shame me, what satisfaction was he gaining, my friend Karen Chetcuti had been murdered and he's inflicting more mental pain on me, something else for me to deal with. He has no compassion, no empathy, just another way to attack me, to hurt me, to push me over the edge. Why?*

These attacks would happen on significant dates such as birthdays, anniversaries and with some of the worst being the first anniversary of my fathers' passing, and the day my best friend was found deceased by her children, which was the 15th January 2017, XXXXX XXXXXXXXXXX XXXXXX XXXXXXXX XX XXXX XXX XXXXXXXXXXX XXXXXX XXXXXXX XX X XXX XXXXXXXXX XXX XXXXXX XXXX X XXX XXXXXX XX XXXX XXX XXX XXXXXX XXX XXXXX XXXXXX. XXX XXX XX XXXXXX XX XXXX XXX XXXXXX XXXXXXX, XXX XX XXXX XXXXXX XXX XXXXXXXX? XX XXXX XXXXX XX XXXX, I had no knowledge of Cathie's passing, it was the next day I was informed, which I frantically left work and went to Cathie's home, hoping it wasn't true. Her death put me into such a deep depression, xxx xxxxxxx xxxx xxxxxxxxxxx xxxxxx xxx xxxxxxx xxx xxxx xxx xxxxxx, X xxxxxxx, xxxxxxxxxxx xxx xxxxxxx. My birthday is a particular day of dread, waiting for bad things to happen, as most of the time, it did.

With the constant terrorising, this meant I had to protect myself, my children which entailed putting in cameras, roller shutters, security doors, a garage and a new car. This has been a massive expense with police only advising me in 2015 to change jobs, get a new car and move house, which in their minds, the stalking would then stop. I did two out of the three things police advised but it made no difference, the attacks were all over Melbourne. My daughter had just started VCE so moving was out of the question, and in all seriousness why should I completely turn my life and my children's lives upside down because this male can't leave me alone, why aren't police advising him to leave me alone or for him to move. I didn't ask for this I just wanted to be left alone.

Sadly I didn't do a great job of protecting my youngest daughter, who was a minor at the age of sixteen when this started, my mother and worst, my best friend, my thoughts are troubling in that how could I have changed all of the events and how they played out and moving wouldn't have changed anything. To lose Cathie, my best friend is a loss I will never recover from, I have truly lost part of my soul. I thought by having all of their home addresses and my daughter's school then her place of employment on my order it would offer some protection, it did not. How naive was I, I truly had no understanding of how little protection my ten-year intervention order ultimately gave my family, my friends and myself.

In 2016 at the age of fifty-two, I also had to find new employment, as my order didn't offer me protection at work as it was his closest shopping centre which to me, seemed more important than my safety. This was a job I had had for close to a decade, when I transferred back to Melbourne in 2013 to care for my ageing parents, I helped build the new store in Craigieburn which also gave me the opportunity to work with some amazing new people. Sadly with Marty Norman constantly hanging around, I couldn't cope with the stress, and resigned. I now work an incredibly long week when you factor in travel, my week is now sixty hours long from the thirty-five hours as management I used to work and I could walk to work in seven minutes. I also have taken a massive pay cut and incur more expenses to travel to and from my place of employment. I am extremely tired and still worried that one day he will find me and terrorise me there and to look for another job at fifty-six, my current age, would add to my already increased stress levels. The increased stress levels have turned my hair white and for my hair to fall out, caused my teeth to snap and has given me shingles, which was extremely painful as it was in my armpit.

To find out that all of my distress has a name, PTSD and major depression, l did attempt suicide in 2015, which left me extremely ill for three days with no one to look after me as everyone I loved was angry at me for these attacks so I felt I had no one to call to take me to hospital, I was completely alone, at least I now understand that from the constant attacks, it has caused me to think and feel this way. Why I constantly think about safety, security, constantly looking over my shoulder or the panic I feel if I see a car like his or his actual car, constantly checking my surroundings or if l think I'm being followed to take random streets and pull over and hide to see who else turns and drives past, to know that it's not normal behaviour but understandable behaviour. The sleeplessness is overwhelming, any noise and I'm up to check my cameras, my doctor has prescribed sleeping tablets, but still I keep waking up to check any noises or why is the dog barking.

The dread I feel every time we are in court, and since 2015 there have been so many court appearances, that I have lost count. I'm always fearful of what is going to happen to me in court as the court system has been extremely difficult as I have never been in trouble before in my life. I've never been in court before in my life. The search for a lawyer was extensive as each lawyer I called they had a conflict, even the Women's Legal Service were unable to help me, I was so distressed, breaking down, asking why, as I'm female he's not. They wouldn't elaborate on the circumstances. I am physically ill before a court hearing as I am that stressed, as I have in the beginning had to represent myself with no legal training or no knowledge on how the court system works. I physically shake going into a court room, today especially, laying out my inner most feelings for everyone to finally know only some of the many things that have been happening to me.

As a result, of my physical and mental state, I don't go out as much as I used to, I don't go to the two venues I was consistently attacked at, I don't see my friends or family as much as I used to, I just don't want to leave my home as my home is safe. It's safe now as I also had a surveillance guy come in and sweep for hidden cameras and bugs, so my home is the only place I can relax in, plus I have fantastic neighbours that are only a text message away at any time day or night. My home is my sanctuary, and at times I am now becoming a hermit, spending weekend after weekend in bed, not wanting to talk or see anyone.

I will never understand why this is happening to me, I was never married to Marty Norman, I never lived with Marty Norman, I never had children with Marty Norman, we only dated for a few months, and I never let him stay overnight as I had a young teenager daughter to think of and her comfort at home was more important than someone I was dating. Marty Norman is actually quite repulsive to me and I curse myself for ever letting him into my life. I wonder where l would be had he not entered my life, would Cathie still be alive, sadly I'm unable to turn back time, so that is a question I will never have the answer to. Cathie was my best friend, my soul sister and my life is completely lost without her. I have no one by my side to talk to any time day or night, so I suffer in silence. I do wonder what Cathie would have thought about how this story has played out, or what she would have thought about the mental illnesses I have now. Marty Norman has completely destroyed my life, I don't know this person, why would you do this to a virtual stranger, why has he inflicted so much pain and anguish on someone he doesn't really know?

I'm asking Your Honour that with the sentence you hand down, that you please consider my sanity over this. I have mentioned being diagnosed with PTSD and major depression and l worry for my future, as his crimes were so egregious, emotionally and mentally violent, I believe that as soon as he's released, he will start back up again. The longer his sentence, the longer peace will live within me otherwise I will never feel at ease, as someone in law enforcement has stated that, having a stalker is like having your own private terrorist, you never know when or how he is going to strike, please Your Honour, I am begging for your assistance to give me back my freedom, my life, my peace and my sanity.

ACKNOWLEDGEMENTS

MY CHILDREN—Sam, Amity and Rhiannon. You guys are my rock, my soul, my life.

Cathie Maney, my BFF. See you on the other side. Until then, I'll miss you forever...

Rebecca Norris—my saviour. Without you, I wouldn't be where I am today. You are a friend for life and thank you for continuing to be on this journey with me.

James R. Fitzgerald—thank you for taking my case. Thank you for still being there for me, for all your guidance and assistance. I am now honoured to call you a friend.

My sister, Michelle, and bro-in-law, Rob. For always being there no matter what. For listening to my rants, my distress and being a voice of reason when I had none.

Maurice and Celeste, for being a rock for Rhiannon and me when Cathie died and then Maurice for opening your home and life to us in Los Angeles for as long as we needed. The four of us had some fabulous times over there.

Special thanks to:

Chris and Tony—the Winelarder, Brighton and Peter and Leeanne—Elwood Food and Wine. You guys went above and beyond. I will forever be grateful.

My beautiful children

Cathie Maney: self-portrait

My 'brother' Trevor, Kylie and their children. A massive thank you for always being 'on call'.

Tess and Cosi—for all those nights I needed company. Your beautiful girls for putting up with me during my messy times.

Mandy, Michael, Robyn G, Lydia, Karen T, Kerryn, Robyn O and Amanda. Thank you for keeping me grounded and entertained.

Daryl B. and band for always having a gig when I needed a distraction. It's been a blast over the past seventeen years; I'm especially grateful for the last ten.

Katie and Mic for your amazing art class. Katie who is now my 'Shazam' twin and Miccy for painting the 'Archibald' of me.

Cheryl Hall, Belinda Hawkins, Simon Winter, Sean Warren, James Fisher and Andrew Cooke—my crew at *Australian Story*: 'To Catch a Stalker'. A massive thank you for telling my story and raising awareness of the effects of stalking. I will be forever grateful.

Hayden Bradford—Protect Victoria

Ed O'Donohue—former Shadow Attorney General and Police Minister

Glenn Corey—staffer for Ed

John Pesutto MP—Member for Hawthorn

Renee Heath MP—Member for Eastern Victoria Region

Lisa Neville—former Police Minister

Jill Hennessy—former Attorney General

Tania Maxwell—former MP, Justice Party

Fiona Patten—former MP, Reason Party

Narelle Fraser—podcaster and former homicide detective

Ron Iddles—former homicide detective

Kathy Kaplan, OAM—founder of Impact

Terry Davis—creator and designer of our Stalking Awareness Day Australia posters and a dear friend. If you like Terry's work, please contact him at www.factoryfloor.net

Darryl and Clare for going above and beyond. Karen K, Nancy, Helly, Kaz, Nishty, Nicole, Marama and Ahn for always being there.

My Dinner Buddies: John, Lynette, Brooke, Eva and Ruby. Also, Marree, Dee Dee and Dimple for making me look fabulous.

Keely, my manager at my corporate gig. For six years you put up with me disappearing at a moment's notice. You would say 'just go' when something happened. Thank you, you are truly a manager who cares for your staff and their wellbeing.

Very special thanks to my amazing Aunty Wilma. You have known me all my life, you were with me the very first time I was in court, and you were there the very last time I was in court. Love you.

For anyone else I haven't mentioned individually, I thank you for being a part of my life and continuing to be so.

Love you all…

And last but not least…

David Limbrick MP, Libertarian Party; Gavin Atkins—staffer and media adviser; Beth Chaney—staffer and social media adviser. There wouldn't be a SADA without you guys.

ABOUT
THE AUTHOR

DI MCDONALD was born in Melbourne in the early 1960s. She moved to Mooroopna after she married, where she built a house with her husband and raised a son and two daughters. After separating in 2009 and finally divorcing in 2013, she decided to move back to Melbourne to help her sister care for their aging parents. Di enjoyed living in Melbourne again, especially as it gave her a chance to be part of the live music scene that she had always loved. She also enjoyed her job as a front-end supervisor at a large new department store in Craigieburn. In late 2014, a chance meeting with a customer in her store changed Di's life forever. She dated this customer for a few months before breaking up with him over his controlling nature. He began to stalk Di and her life turned into a nightmare of anxiety and apprehension. Years of battling through the courts saw her stalker finally jailed. Today, Di is an advocate for stalking law reform and is promoting awareness around stalking and the dangerous potential of this insidious and misunderstood crime. Di is currently living at an undisclosed location. Di's beloved dog Roxy has passed away suddenly, but her children remain her rock, continue to support her, and are now flourishing with their own lives.

LEFT Roxy 2011—2025

RIGHT First holiday in peace:
with Michelle in Daylesford in 2021

Stalking Awareness Day Australia
24th May
www.sada.au

RIP STEVE
(1958–2025)

WE MET WHEN we were in our fourties, now we're in our sixties.

Thank you for being with me when my Dad passed away.

Thank you for coming with me to the party to end all parties: Models 2015. Your comment of the night was 'Elton John has arrived'—too funny, it was my old Show Ads client, Charles Billich. We then spent hours with Charles, Christa and Paul.

Thank you for dropping everything to meet me at Cathie's then meeting every year with Maurice and Celeste on Cath's anniversary.

Thank you for being there for me when my Mum died.

Thank you for being there through the years of bullshit I went through with stalker.

Thank you for making me laugh, especially when we nearly burnt down the factory.

Thank you for wanting to teach me to weld, and more recently to teach me to paddle board. You can now fly high with Cathie and Emit, maybe teach them to paddle board. Now that would be hilarious.

Love ya guts.
My final word...slapppppppppp